D1473056

MOTIVATING MILLENNIALS

HOW TO RECOGNIZE, RECRUIT AND RETAIN THE NEXT GENERATION OF LEADERS

Ryan Avery and **James Goodnow**

Copyright © 2017 by Ryan Avery and G. James Goodnow III
All rights reserved. This book or any portion thereof
may not be reproduced or used in any manner whatsoever
without the express written permission of the publisher
except for the use of brief quotations in a book review.

Printed in the United States of America
First Printing, 2017

ISBN 978-0- 692-84145- 7

Cover design by Jon Firman
Edits by PJ Dempsey and Evelyn Fazio

AveryToday, Inc.
PO BOX 1516
Englewood, CO 80150

Find us online and learn more at:
MotivatingMillennialsBook.com

For The Triangles

ACKNOWLEDGEMENTS

No book is ever written by one person. It takes a sea of thought leaders, researchers, editors, family members who stay up way too late to listen to us read aloud our newly crafted paragraphs, along with designers, coordinators and others to make sure we deliver the product that will serve as the premiere resource to help others.

In this case, we want the resource to be all about showing Baby Boomer executives how to motivate Millennial employees. We are proud of this book because we are proud of the people who helped make it happen!

Thank you to the extraordinarily talented Keridwen Cornelius for helping us put our thoughts, ideas, and words into sentences that people actually want to read. Thank you to our backbone Terence Murnin for keeping everything organized and flowing on time. Thank you to Mindy "Mimi" Mahoney, PJ Dempsey and Evelyn Fazio for your editing skills and reading the book more times than we thought you would. Thank you to Jon Firman for your amazing design work and formatting.

Thank you to those who are taking the time to read this book; we don't want the strategies shared in these pages to sit on a shelf; we want them shared, executed, and incorporated into your daily business habits so you can grow your business and so that people our age can feel inspired to go to work every day.

Thank you to our smart, talented, and amazing wives who watched us stay up way too late and wake up way too early to meet our deadlines. Thank you to our children for letting us read chapter edits to you for bedtime stories rather than Dr. Seuss or J.K. Rowling.

Thank you to our friends and family who shared articles, videos, and books to use to enrich this book. Thank you for helping us make this book happen. Thank you for motivating us!

MOTIVATING MILLENNIALS

HOW TO RECOGNIZE, RECRUIT AND RETAIN THE NEXT GENERATION OF LEADERS

Ryan Avery and James Goodnow

TABLE OF CONTENTS

Introduction 10

Chapter 1 - Reconsidering: Understanding Millennials 13

Generational Shapes™ 15

Triangles Hiring Circles 20

Higher Position vs. New Position 22

The Myth That Corporate Success Equals Job Security 23

Few Options vs. Overwhelming Options 25

Work-life Balance vs. Work-life Blend 28

Own vs. Experience 30

Communication vs. Communication 32

Real-World Story: Boomer Perspective 35

Real-World Story: Millennial Perspective 38

Chapter 2 - Recruiting: Finding Millennials 41

A Tale of Three Shoe Companies 42

Before the Interview: A Circular Design 45

Case Study: Rackspace 47

Active Recruiting 49

During the Interview: A Circular Approach 55

After the Interview: Circular Hiring 58

Real-World Story: Millennial Perspective 60

Chapter 3 - Retaining: Keeping Millennials 63

Disregard Stereotypes 64

Motivation: Shift from Compensation to Cause 66

Culture: Shift from Competition to Collaboration 70

Career Goals: Shift from the Corporate Ladder to a Seat at the Table   74

Incentives and Feedback: Shift From Annual to Incremental 79

Schedules: Shift from Work-Life Balance to Work-Life Blend 83

Real-World Story: Millennial Perspective 86

Chapter 4 - Realizing: Motivating and Promoting Millennials   89

Communicating with Millennials 91

Make Mentoring More Circular 100

Consider Various Types of Millennial Mentoring Programs 101

Identifying Leaders in the Circular Company 105

Multicultural Millennials with EI 109

Training: Managers vs. Motivators 110

Real-World Story: Gen Xer Perspective 116

Introduction

Many books and articles about Millennials start with this warning: By 2030, Millennials will take over 75 percent of the workforce. They're coming, and if you don't learn to manage them, they'll leave and your company will lose.

This warning makes you think the world is bracing for an alien invasion of jeans-wearing, smartphone-wielding selfie takers. As members of the Millennial generation ourselves, we're here to tell those of you who are Baby Boomers and Gen Xers that it's not true. In fact, we'd like to debunk these misconceptions.

First, Millennials are not a threat. Instead, we can be your biggest asset. We're an enthusiastic, hardworking, purpose-driven group of innovative thinkers. Contrary to popular belief, we aren't anti-Corporate America but the structure of most businesses today thwarts our natural strengths rather than providing the environment we need to thrive.

Second, Millennials *can* be managed, but it's not our first choice. We prefer to be motivated. When we're motivated, we actually manage ourselves, and this self-management is what allows us to accomplish great things for your company.

This book will explain how to motivate Millennials and show you how to capitalize on the great potential of our often-maligned generation.

This book will explain how to motivate Millennials and show you how to capitalize on the great potential of our often-maligned generation. To do this, we'll explain how to get past the stereotypes and explain who Millennials really are. You'll gain a new perspective as we shine a light on the family dynamics that shaped us. If you're a Boomer, we learned our values from you. If you're a Gen Xer, you share many of these same values. We'll also explore how to create the business structures and strategies that work to recruit, retain, and promote the best Millennials. You'll also learn how you can inspire us to do more and be more, how to realize our full potential and capitalize on it for your company.

If you're wondering if your company has to cater to Millennials, the answer is no. But if you don't, you'll lose out in the end. This book will show you why Millennial-friendly practices are great for business, and why these changes to accommodate Millennials are necessary in a fast-changing economy driven by knowledge and innovation.

Of course, we must remember that each person within a generation is different, as are their families and the circumstances in which they grew up. With that in mind, we believe our strategies will help you bridge the generation gap with the unique individuals in your organization.

Today people are living and working longer than ever before. This is the first time that so many people of different generations have had the opportunity to work together. And, thanks to technology, they are doing so in a variety of ways. We view this historic situation as a great opportunity and not as an overwhelming obstacle – which is unfortunately often the case. Knowledge sharing that encourages the cross-pollination of ideas can spark major innovation – if the different generations can learn how to collaborate in a way that capitalizes on their strengths and compensates for their weaknesses.

We can create successful companies in which individuals from every generation are motivated and inspired to do their best. The goal is not to just get along in the workplace; rather, it's to know, understand, and inspire each other along with growing the bottom line.

CHAPTER 1

•

Reconsidering:
Understanding Millennials

How do you describe a Millennial? If you're like most Baby Boomers and Gen Xers, perhaps words like *entitled*, *lazy*, and *narcissistic* come to mind. But it's our hope that you'll come away from this book thinking instead of words like *innovative*, *caring*, and *open-minded*. Indeed, it's the goal of this first chapter to change your perception of Millennials and to debunk the myths associated with this generation. So let's begin by sharing how Millennials came to be perceived in this negative light.

We do want to make it clear that our book, like any other written about generational differences, will make broad generalizations. Millennials, according to the Pew Research Center, comprise the generation of 75.4 million people born between 1981 and 1997. It's as unfair to generalize and make blanket statements about our generation as it is to generalize about the 74.9 million Baby Boomers or the 65 million Gen Xers who followed them. This does not mean the generations shouldn't be examined; it means care should be used when doing so because the observations are not always universal and exceptions can always be found.

To understand Millennials, we can't start by examining what happens at the conference table in the workplace. Instead, we must go back to the family dinner table where we first learned how to socialize.

Baby Boomers
(1945 - 1964)*

Gen Xers
(1965 - 1979)*

Millennials
(1980 - 2000)*

* the dates above will be used in this book to define the generations.

Generational Shapes™

To a large degree, everything we learned by interacting with our family forms the basis of how we interact with the world around us. Our relationship with our parents and siblings gets projected onto our interactions with our bosses and our coworkers. The hierarchy we experienced as children is mirrored in our institutions. Boomers, Gen Xers, and Millennials all grew up in families and in different times in history that shaped us in very different ways. This is what we mean by *Generational Shapes™*.

THE TRIANGLE

- Create an empire
- Parents dictated
- Work ethic is 9 -5
- Generalized rewards
- Leaders defined by IQ

Baby Boomers typically grew up in a pyramid-shaped household, with Mom and Dad at the top, functioning as the dictators of a miniature - empire. Therefore, we choose the triangle as the Baby Boomers' Generational Shape™.

Parents of this generation usually sat at the head of the dinner table, where they dominated the conversation in content and tone. When they told you to do your chores or practice the piano, you did it because they made it clear that there was no choice. And it was often followed with "Because I said so."

Baby Boomers grew up in homes with parents who lived through the Great Depression, World War II and the Cold War. They knew what it meant to live in uncertain times and to do without. For Baby Boomers' parents, it made sense that saving for their retirement or for their children's college education took precedence over buying their kids trendy shoes or expensive cars. Their parents had worked hard and most expected their children to do the same; to earn their keep, and in many cases, to contribute toward college – no questions asked.

Boomers knew exactly where they belonged in this triangle: at the bottom. But the benefit was that once they landed a job and worked their way up through a pyramid-shaped company hierarchy, they could have their own family and claim a place at the top of their own triangle.

This triangle mindset may have launched many a successful career, but it didn't mean everyone liked it. Talk to Boomers and you'll find many who resented when their parents told them what to do without explanation. Many in this generation also resented the powers-that-be who brought the world to the brink of nuclear destruction and drafted young men, many against their will, to fight in Vietnam.

It was also members of this generation who climbed the corporate ladder, or pyramid, while wondering why they were devoting their life to working for "the man."

Because Baby Boomers couldn't shift the workplace paradigm, or change the government structure, they instead transformed the family. This meant that Boomers could parent in the way they wish they had been parented. This grass-roots change meant they could change the world through their children. When younger Boomers gave birth to the Millennials, together they created the circle household.

THE CIRCLE

- Create a community
- Parents explained
- Work ethic is results based
- Customized rewards
- Leaders defined by I WILL

The circular household is not a triangular dictatorship. There is no head – it's a democracy. Mom and Dad didn't mandate what you did. Instead they acted as leaders who asked for and valued the input of their family. This is why we choose the circle as the Millennials' Generational Shape™.

Parents of Millennials often asked for their opinions. This new generation was encouraged to express their thoughts and ideas and Millennials delighted in being able to be forthright. This was also the first generation born into a world dominated by technology. The rapid pace of technological change created a unique situation where children often knew much more than their parents about the new digital world.

Boomers didn't choose to make demands of their Millennial children. Instead, they opted to explain, negotiate, and incentivize. Everyday chores often evolved into money making opportunities. The maddening phrase, "because I told you so" evolved into a request and a rationale "Could you clean up your toys, please? I need you to tidy up because we want the house to look nice for company."

Millennials were generally encouraged to "be yourself." Because their parents often had their views dismissed as silly or impractical, many Millennials grew up being taught that everybody's feelings were valid and that uniqueness was to be celebrated. They tended to be enrolled in every possible activity - from gymnastics to robotics, drama club to investment club - all meant to encourage them to find their calling and believe they could be whatever they wanted to be.

As a group, Millennials grew up believing they were special and that it was possible to find a career that perfectly matched that specialness. It could even be one where they could change the world and be happy doing it.

Then it happened! Millennials grew up and left these cozy, safe, nurturing circular households and expected to live in a circular world. Instead, they were thrust into a workplace created and run by the previous two generations, most of whom grew up in triangular households and as a result created triangular workplaces. It was a shock – for all three generations.

THE SQUARE

- Wants to create **both**
- Parents did **both**
- **Both** work ethics
- Ok with **both** types of rewards
- Ok with **both** leaders

Familial and cultural changes tend to happen gradually. Therefore, it makes sense that Gen Xers possess qualities of both the Boomers and Millennials. For this reason, their outlook falls between the triangle and the circle and makes their Generational Shape™ the square.

When Gen Xers were growing up, the phrase "latch-key kids" came into being because so many of them got home before their parents. This situation helped drive the Gen Xers' independent streak. So, like Boomers, they didn't rely on frequent feedback, but made their own independent decisions. Yet they don't tip completely to the Boomer side as they also share in the Millennials' freewheeling spirit. Like Millennials, they're often adept at technology and using social media. But growing up in the time before cell phones and email means that, like Boomers, they don't text when there's an opportunity to meet and chat face-to-face.

As you can see, Gen Xers are in the best position to bridge the gap between Boomers and Millennials.

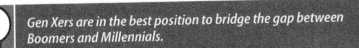

Gen Xers are in the best position to bridge the gap between Boomers and Millennials.

Think of Gen Xers as the "Switzerland" of the generational clash. If you belong to this generation, chances are you'll recognize yourself in the middle as we further explore the differences between triangular and circular thinking.

DIFFERENT GENERATIONS, DIFFERENT ATTITUDES

Now it's time to see how these differences play out in the workplace with two of the generations experiencing the time before computers, cell phones, and social media, and another generation not being able to imagine life without them. And how these different generations handle specific, and sometimes rigid rules, affect how they behave on the job and relate to supervisors and coworkers. Indeed, a whole industry has sprung up with books and workshops devoted to this very subject.

Triangles Hiring Circles

Most workplace clashes are created when triangles hire circles. Boomers and Millennials are too far apart in age and work experience to fall into an easy pattern of working together. They grew up in different worlds. As a manager, you may have experienced this firsthand if you hired Millennials who began the job bursting with ideas for improving the company and had absolutely no problem freely offering their opinions to upper management. But this is not how it was for Boomers. When Boomers were coming up through the ranks, everyone had their place and you would never think of talking to your boss's boss or breaking the chain of command. Boomers respected the triangle and understood that they had to climb the ladder or pyramid.

Why is it that Millennials can be so frustrating to Boomers? Let us explain, and we mean literally *"us"* because we, the authors, are Millennials.

If we Millennials think we have a good idea and want to make sure it's heard by those who can actually make it happen (no matter what their rank), we think it's perfectly okay to share it. It's not because we're arrogant upstarts – well, some of us are (there are jerks in every generation). It's because, from day one, the contributions we made to our family were valued. We understood that, although our parents were equipped with the knowledge and experience we lacked, we also knew things about smartphones, social media, and computers that they didn't. We got used to being helpful members of a team and helping each other for the greater good. As a result, we naturally think a good idea is worth pursuing, whether it comes from an intern or the CEO.

Conversely, we think an ineffective strategy should be ditched, even if it's the boss's idea. This is often the trigger that sets off conflict with colleagues not part of our generation. For example, statements like, "This is the way the company has always done it," do not make sense to us and we react accordingly. It's not that we don't respect authority. It's that we don't respect decisions without rationale from people in authority because we were taught the value of questioning and providing explanations.

We believe that if someone can't give a good reason for doing something, there probably isn't one.

It can seem ironic that Boomers popularized the practice of questioning authority and never trusting anyone over 30. Despite that, Boomers were often taught to obey those in authority because of their triangular upbringing. Many Boomers may have grumbled to themselves and gone along with the status quo to keep their job and climb the corporate pyramid. Getting regular raises and promotions aren't a guarantee in today's corporate world, and we Millennials aren't necessarily interested in climbing the pyramid anyway. The ultimate difference is that we're not trying to inherit an empire; what we want is to create a community.

Higher Position vs. New Position
A New Way of Thinking

Triangular thinkers often believe that rising through the ranks translates into a movement in their thinking. Unfortunately, to us Millennials as Circular thinkers, that approach feels like stagnation. Circular thinkers, true to our shape, want to roll around through the different ranks. What's often hard for those who came before us to accept is that we are the most educated and global-minded generation that's ever lived, just as the Boomers were to the generation before them. We thrive on consistently being challenged and want to expand our orbit so we can keep learning.

Like most of the young people of the generations before us, we're idealists. But more than any generation, we bring that idealism into the workplace. What we want is to change business to be more inclusive to Millennials by being more circular in design. We want to be heard. We want to feel valued.

> We want to feel like we are at the table. That's more important to us than a promotion, and it makes it easier for us to speak up and challenge the status quo within the organization. It also lets us rock the boat because we're not biding our time until the next promotion.

We want to feel like we are at the table. That's more important to us than a promotion, and it makes it easier for us to speak up and challenge the status quo within the organization. It also lets us rock the boat because we're not biding our time until the next promotion.

It's this behavior that we believe makes us stand out in a hyper-competitive world. We fear that if we don't stand out, we'll be lost in the fray. We also believe that by taking initiative and saying what we think, we will help improve the company and feel fulfilled. In turn, we expect to be rewarded with opportunities that will give us a wider scope for our imagination. And that, to us, is success.

The Myth That Corporate Success Equals Job Security

Between the Boomer heyday and today, the ties that bind employer and employee have gradually loosened and come apart. Today, most people don't hesitate to change jobs or move to another city for a better opportunity. In some companies, this tendency may label workers as ones who are not serious about their job, thereby making them expendable. But consider this: Millennials grew up seeing our parents, relatives, and their colleagues and friends get laid off despite years of dedicated service. We heard them lament over the loss of pensions and health insurance. The message that came across to us was loud and clear: Nothing is guaranteed.

We also experienced it firsthand as we launched our own careers during the Great Recession's mass layoffs. Many of us already have stories of interviewing with companies that folded a month later. We earned diplomas in what we thought were vibrant industries that suddenly faltered and died out.

When we picture individuals at the top of triangular companies, we don't always see role models. Instead, we all too often see triangular businesses run by the likes of Bernie Madoff and Wall Street investment bankers with undeserved bonuses. By contrast, we Millennials admire those industries and companies that we feel are doing things right. (See Chapter 2 for examples.)

Because we don't consider the corporate pyramid as stable and safe, we feel better relying on our own initiative and building our own brand. And to us, it's also more interesting.

Because we don't consider the corporate pyramid as stable and safe, we feel better relying on our own initiative and building our own brand. And to us, it's also more interesting.

Few Options vs. Overwhelming Options

We'd like to ask Baby Boomers to think back to their 20's when they launched their careers. What choices were available back then? Chances are you probably felt pressure from your parents to choose among the limited acceptable occupations available at the time. In the pre-Internet era, today's wide variety of job possibilities just didn't exist. For women or people of color, society limited their choices even more. Past generations also felt the gravitational pull of their hometowns and to stay near family and friends. Keep in mind that it wasn't that long ago when a telephone call to another state was considered "long distance" and was expensive. And back then, job hunting was done by scanning the want ads in the local paper, attending a career fair, or being recruited on a college campus.

Then, enter technology as a game changer. Technology has created whole new industries, and thousands of new types of jobs, along with a global economy. We now have so much more freedom and choice. Pioneering technological and scientific advances have opened a vast number of new careers around the country, as well as the world. That has sent individuals and families scattering far and wide.

Today, Millennials have a litany of occupations to choose from that didn't exist 10 or 20 years ago – across the country and the planet. These "new" jobs include app developer, podcast host, urban agriculturalist, chief listening officer, market research data miner, 3-D architectural visualizer, 3-D printing specialist, social media manager, director of vibe, information security analyst, medical coder, space lawyer, sustainability expert, user experience designer, and freelance drone operator, among many others.

Finding those jobs has even gotten more creative. We have an onslaught of outlets: Jobs2Careers.com, Monster.com, Mediabistro.com, LinkedIn.com, each company's website, Facebook groups, Craigslist, Twitter shout-outs, and the list goes on and evolves.

THE DOWNSIDE OF TOO MANY OPTIONS

Technology and choice are great to have, but having too many options also comes with a downside.

Technology and choice are great to have, but having too many options also comes with a downside. Being bombarded with an overwhelming number of options does affect the mind. For proof, let's consider what goes into the buying of jam. Yes, jam!

In 2000, a now famous study about "choice paralysis" was published by psychologists Sheena Iyengar and Mark Lepper of Columbia and Stanford universities. The researchers set up two displays of jam in a gourmet grocery store, one consisted of six varieties and the other, 24 varieties. They then offered coupons to the hundreds of shoppers who sampled the products in the store.

Their results were surprising: 30 percent of shoppers who sampled from the six jars bought jam and most were happy with their choices. But 97 percent of people who encountered the 24 jam display were so overwhelmed by the number of options that they walked away empty-handed. Of the 3 percent who did buy jam from the larger display, most regretted their choice. And it's precisely this overwhelming abundance of options in the job

market that affects Millennials. Here's why:
- FOMO (Fear of Missing Out) (Yes it's a real thing!)
- Dissatisfaction with their decisions

But there's an even bigger factor at work, and that is the significance of these abundant options. The Greatest Generation and Silent Generation (the generations before Boomers) viewed jobs as a way to make money, and they looked to their families and their free time for personal fulfillment. They passed this philosophy on to their Baby Boomer children, who started out by adopting this mindset but gradually changed it. Boomers, in turn, sought more fulfillment from their careers and wanted their children, students, and protégés to adopt this as well. This attitude encouraged Millennials to discover our true calling – or the career equivalent of a soulmate. We were told to find the perfect occupation for our unique personality and talents. We were also told that we could be anything we wanted.

But, there's an unintended downside to this inspirational message because it puts pressure on making the perfect career choice. For many Millennials, a job is not a paycheck; rather, it defines our purpose in life. So we're often haunted by the thought that without the right job, we have no true purpose. We're supposed to match our personality with a "soulmate" job. But as Walt Whitman said, "We contain multitudes." For which part of our personality should we search for and find a compatible job?

Think about this dilemma when you want to criticize a Millennial for not finding a job. Because we believe we have a wide range of job options which could be right for us, every time we search through a job site or read about a burgeoning field, a different part of us gets excited about the possibilities.

Writing cover letters for various jobs can feel like coping with a multiple personality disorder. One day we tell a potential employer our true passion is the environment; the next day it's entrepreneurship, or children's education, or the food industry. We're not disingenuous; we're just multi-passionate. And once we do choose, we're like the people who bought one of those 24 jams – nagged with regret and buyer's remorse because we had to reject so many other options.

When we switch jobs or fields too quickly, we are accused of fearing commitment, or worse, of lacking a work ethic or even not caring. Most of us do have a work ethic, as well as drive and passion. But we also have so many options that we can't decide where to focus. We care so much that we're actually paralyzed when we have to choose.

To help Millennials direct their drive toward your company, see Chapters 3 and 4.

Work-life Balance vs. Work-life Blend

Baby Boomers grew up in a time when "don't take the office home with you" was the prevailing wisdom. And it made sense for a number of reasons. When you're a triangular thinker building work and home empires, you want to construct those empires based on separate sets of values. When you seek a paycheck from work and fulfillment from your free time, you want to keep those aspects of your life separate. Plus, in the pre-laptop era, "taking the office home" would mean lugging a heavy briefcase full of papers and files.

That vision of work-life balance sliced up the day like a pie: a sliver of family time in the morning, then a large wedge of work during the rest of the day, and then another helping of family time in the evening.

Technology has obliterated those separations. Email and cell phone calls have increasingly encroached on personal time to the extent that we are all finding it challenging to navigate this fast-changing world. But we Millennials approach it from our own, unique perspective.

Millennials are digital natives who are used to being constantly connected to our friends, coworkers, bosses, families, teachers, and an entire virtual world. In our circular minds, our work and our personal life are as interconnected as the World Wide Web. We seek fulfillment and enjoyment from both, so we don't need to divide them in our schedules.

In fact, we want to take the office home: 75 percent of us would like to work remotely some or all the time, according to the 2016 Deloitte Millennial Survey. We prefer a flexible schedule that allows us to hit the gym in the middle of the day and stay late at the office or to complete a project in a cafe. Maybe take a Tuesday to scuba dive and instead work on a Saturday. We think the focus should be on accomplishing work goals, not filling up hours in a rigid schedule.

The Boomer desire for work-life balance vs. the Millennial desire for work-life blend is causing a culture clash in the workplace that's a problem for both generations. Today, you have some people who want flexible schedules, while others must work jobs with traditional hours, such as bank tellers. But there are solutions that could work for everyone. (See Chapter 3.)

Own vs. Experience

An interesting perspective on generational differences can be found by comparing the wedding registry of Boomer couples and Millennial couples. Boomers registered for china, silverware, bar cabinets, and other home furnishings. Millennials register for surfing lessons, mixology classes, and help funding their Hawaiian honeymoon. The difference is simple: many of us want to collect experiences, not possessions.

Boomers experienced their future following a distinct plan and divided it into distinct sections, kind of like the workday. They would spend years earning a living, raising a family, and establishing a home. Then they would retire and do all the traveling and recreation they had put off for years. To accomplish this, they would need to keep moving up in their job, take out a 30-year mortage to own a home and hope that their 401(k) or pension wouldn't disappear.

Millennials saw people's retirement plans wrecked by the Great Recession. We witnessed the housing crisis and then the surging price of starter homes. Many of us are already mired in debt: college tuition costs have risen by 1,225 percent since 1978, according to the Bureau of Labor Statistics. It doesn't help that we worked unpaid internships to get future job opportunities, only to find ourselves in low-paying jobs with stagnant salaries. We typically can't afford the house with the two-car garage. But it's not necessarily on our wish list anyway.

We grew up with the world at our fingertips, constantly tempting us: YouTube videos of bungee jumpers in New Zealand, Facebook photos of friends' trips to Iceland or Instagrams posts of Ironman competitions. We're the most ethnically diverse generation in history, so we're in touch with a variety of cultures. We were raised during a foodie revolution, with culinary adventures on every corner.

For Millennials, it's *carpe diem*. We don't want to put off traveling until our golden years, only to find those years taken away. We'd rather rent an apartment and spend our money on adventures and travel. And that flexibility gives us the option of moving to Portland next year if we feel like it. We can't stand the idea of being stuck in one place. To us, the words "forever home" sound about as scary as the Bates Motel. And we hate signing long-term contracts. Can't we just rent?

This perspective often gets misunderstood by previous generations, says Patricia Wyrod, a tech attorney in San Francisco who frequently works with Millennials. "They're not motivated by the same carrot and stick that previous generations were. I think that sometimes people from other generations see that and say things like 'You don't care about buying a house? OK, well, you have no ambition and you're a slacker.' Instead, what I see is that they're very ambitious when it comes to personal freedom and to not be owned and controlled by the man, to not be trapped in a social framework. They want a rich life, a life filled with depth of experience."

Because of this, Millennials view work differently than generations past. Boomers who had to make the mortgage and car payment were more inclined to be anchored to stable jobs. We

Millennials aren't tied to houses and large-scale possessions, and many of us are putting off having kids. So we're more flexible in the way we approach work. We might take more time finding the right position. Or we might seek out a contract job for a month and then leave for a month. We're also motivated by different goals in our jobs. We'll explore how understanding this can help you in Chapter 3.

Communication vs. Communication

Let's play word association. If we say "communication" and you're a Boomer, you'll probably conjure a face-to-face conversation or a phone call. If you're a Millennial, you might imagine texting or Slack or Facebook, or FaceTime or a chat over a latte.

Obviously, each generation views communication differently. Among Americans younger than 50, texting has become the most frequently used form of communication, according to a 2014 Gallup poll. Most people older than 50 prefer phone calls. If the poll had asked about in-person conversations, those would no doubt rank even higher. Boomers and Gen Xers focus on the method of communication and rue the lost art of conversation. Millennials focus on the act of communication and feel it can take lots of effective forms.

> Boomers and Gen Xers focus on the method of communication and often rue the lost art of conversation. Millennials focus on the act of communication and feel it can take lots of effective forms.

But our generations also have a lot in common. We're all overwhelmed by the multitude of communication forms we use in our work life. Even for digital natives, it's exhausting to text, Facebook, Instagram, Tweet, IM, FaceTime, email, call and have in-person meetings.

We're all struggling to acquire the skills necessary to master each medium. A few decades ago, if you wanted to boost your communication game, you read Dale Carnegie's *How to Win Friends and Influence People*, which is packed with tips on improving conversation. Now, you have to learn email and texting etiquette, Instagram effectiveness, Facebook Live skills, LinkedIn presentation, Twitter versus Snapchat audience optimization, and the five other things that were invented while you were learning those. A manager can no longer tell an employee to improve their communication skills. Which one of the dozens do they mean?

We also all waste a lot of energy navigating generation gaps and personal preferences. To ask someone a question, we have to consider several options: Do they prefer Internet, or text, or a phone call? Is Facebook much less professional than email, even though the messages end up in the same inbox? Will using an exclamation point make me sound immature, or will not using it make me sound like a zombie? Why am I sending this epic email instead of walking down the hall to talk? Did I just hit Reply All?

Millennials also typically communicate in a more casual manner than people from previous generations, which often gets misinterpreted as disrespectful or unprofessional. Patricia Wyrod says she's learned to appreciate this communication style for what it is. Millennials "really actually value being warm, friendly, kicked back, laid back," she says. "There's really a premium put on saying, 'What's up? How are you? Hey, that sounds great. I'd love to look at that with you. Cool. Can't wait.' Previous generations considered talking that way as low-power styles of communication." Working with Millennials has "made me feel that it's okay to be who I am," Wyrod says. "If you have a pleasant, friendly affect and you're a woman, sometimes people confuse warmth with incompetence. I'm actually a super nice person. I'm also bubbly and I can be kind of goofy. But I'm also very smart, hardworking, and competent. I'm the person who wants to give you a hug before we start work, or ask how your kids are doing before we start a meeting. And I think Millennials have had a huge influence on me."

In the end, it comes down to understanding each other if we want to succeed in a supportive environment that inspires us all.

In the end, it comes down to understanding each other if we want to succeed in a supportive environment that inspires us all. We all want our lives and our work to have purpose, and the basis for that is communication, whether casual or formal, in-person or virtual.

Call us optimistic, but we believe the generations are not so different and that we all can work effectively and well together.

Real-World Story: Boomer Perspective
Patricia Wyrod, Tech and Startup Attorney

"I'm very impressed with them... I think Millennials have had a huge influence on me."

Born the last year of the Baby Boom, Patricia Wyrod launched her legal career when Gordon Gekko-esque greed had swept the nation. She worked at a prominent international law firm where attorneys flashed status symbols – Rolex watches, European suits, fast cars – to indicate their place on the triangular hierarchy. The very few women lawyers on staff were not allowed to wear pants, and Wyrod had to suppress her naturally bubbly personality to be more "professional."

So when she began working as a startup attorney in Silicon Valley, she was surprised at how different it was to work with Millennials. "I'm very impressed with them," says Wyrod, 52. "I really enjoy working with them and have found myself starting to adopt some of their attitudes in my own life… I think a lot of people in my generation verbalize a lot of stereotypical prejudices about Millennials that can look correct on the surface. But when you get to know these people, there's so much more going on."

So what has Wyrod learned from working with Millennials?

FIRST, MILLENNIALS' CASUAL STYLE DOES NOT MEAN DISRESPECT: "They're not actually interested in status and elitism in the same way [previous generations were]. They have a very casual lifestyle… They're not afraid to come to work in jeans and track shoes. It can be interpreted by older people as being disrespectful, or like this ambitionless person who is disinterested in climbing the ladder, like they're not going to try hard. What I think it is, instead, is this really strong commitment to egalitarianism. They're not interested in saving up enough money to buy a Rolex. They're not interested in being better than the next guy. A lot of the cars, and the watches, and the expensive French-collared shirts are about signaling status. But Millennials are not driven by a need to walk into a room and establish that they're the higher status person."

SECOND, WANTING WORK-LIFE BLEND IS NOT LAZINESS: "A lot of them do have really strong boundaries around work, in that they will work 9:00 to 5:30, but no weekends. It's not laziness. They're leaving work because they want to be with their friends, and they want to have experiences, and they want to be with their community. They want to have balanced, enriched lives. They really have so much maturity around what work is for, and what the role of work in one's life is. It's made me really rethink how much of my own ambition is more about striving just because of the generation I grew up in, and letting go of the goals of striving and saying, 'What I really want to do is do cool things with cool people I enjoy spending time with.' I think I never felt I was entitled to ask for that from work until I started working with Millennials.

THIRD, MILLENNIALS CAN BE INSPIRING: A lot of [Millennial] women are so relaxed and comfortable with being women. They dress the way they want to dress… They have this total lack of self-consciousness about their gender. They're just not that eager to follow all the corporate rules and that really makes them look empowered. I find that really, really inspirational. Being able to go visit the clients and wear whatever I want, and just to relax and be myself… It's actually okay to come into the office of some high-tech company with close to $59 million in funding and ask, 'How are you? How was the weekend?' It's okay just to be a warm person because [Millennials] value that."

FOURTH: POSTING ON SOCIAL MEDIA DOESN'T MEAN MILLENNIALS ARE NARCISSISTIC: "It does look really selfish and narcissistic on the surface, but that is not what I see. I actually see people who are really interested in being part of a community that is not a hierarchal community; it's an egalitarian community. Social media is an incredible leveler. When we get to know someone through their Instagram feed, you can't see what neighborhood they live in or what kind of car they drive. I think they want to engage, and they want to be in constant contact with each other. And it's just really fun to share. They're just doing it for the joy of it."

Real-World Story: Millennial Perspective
Jenny Poon
Founder, CO+HOOTS

"If you channel Millennials in the right direction, they are 100 times more efficient than any other generation, and they will run 100 times faster."

Jenny Poon comes from a long line of bold and enterprising people. During the Sino-Japanese War, her grandparents escaped China and settled in Vietnam. Then the Vietnam War broke out, forcing her future parents to flee, separately, to the United States. Her teenaged mother sold seats on a small boat, using the finder's fees to buy herself a spot on the Pacific voyage. They both ended up in Minnesota. They married, had Poon and her siblings, and launched a series of restaurants.

Clearly, Poon's story is not typical of Millennials. Yet she has many typical Millennial qualities. She's entrepreneurial: She founded CO+HOOTS, which has been called the most innovative co-working space in the country, and built it into a community of 250 businesses. She fosters an atmosphere of collaboration rather than competition. And she doesn't like to manage her staff, but instead empowers "every single person to be an innovator, to lead and own their own piece of things."

Here are some things Poon has learned about her fellow Millennials in the modern workplace:

FIRST, ON THE STEREOTYPING OF MILLENNIALS: "It's funny, because I did believe in a lot of the stereotypes when I first started my business. I only hire Millennials now, and I think my first hire really opened my eyes. Basically, I believed she was entitled. Sometimes I thought she was lazy. But I realized it wasn't that she was lazy. She just wasn't passionate about the work she was doing. So I do think, if you channel Millennials in the right direction, they are 100 times more efficient than any other generation, and they will run 100 times faster. They will be 100 times more effective. But the minute you point them in a direction that they are not driven by, that's when you will run into the hurdles. So you do have to spend more time nurturing your employees. But your payout is much greater. All of my staff, I think, is super excited to be here. Everyone here is on time. I've never said that you can't be late. I've never set a strict schedule. They kind of self-police each other, which is great. I hate management."

SECOND, ON MILLENNIALS' DEVELOPMENT TIMELINE: There's a belief that "Millennials are the first generation to not be as wealthy as their parents. I'd challenge that in saying that they might not be as wealthy as their parents at a certain age. There's this new phase that I think happens with the Millennial generation that didn't happen with the past generation, and that's a phase of discovery. So you go through high school, and you go through college just like your parents did. Then you go through a discovery phase, whereas your parents went right into jobs, family, home. I think that, once you hit your 30s, your knowledge-gathering is a lot more than your parents had, which then allows you to channel your passions and your strengths into something that's going to further you."

THIRD, ON FOSTERING COLLABORATION RATHER THAN COMPETITION IN THE WORKPLACE: "Seeing somebody really creative next to me makes me want to be just as creative. It promotes and challenges me to be better. In our space, we have four different designers and five different web-development teams. They always compete on projects, but they also come together and brainstorm solutions for their own clients' projects. It's not really competition; it's trying to figure out how we differentiate from each other, because there's always something different."

FOURTH, ON HELPING HER MILLENNIAL STAFF – AND HERSELF – FIND PASSION AT WORK: "When I wake up, I can't wait to see my daughter. I hear her in the other room and I just jump out of bed and go play with her. How do you have that same reaction with the work that you do? You should be able to. There's no reason you shouldn't. There's gonna be bad days, right? There's days when my daughter is grumpy and angry, and not listening to anything I say. But, for the most part, she's awesome. So I want work to feel that way. And if you're not feeling that way, how do we fix it? Is there something we can shift you to where your energy is better spent, or is it honestly that we need to help you find a better position outside of our company? And we're happy to do that too." (We'll discuss Poon's method for connecting her employees with their passions and helping them achieve their goals in Chapter 4.)

CHAPTER 2

•

Recruiting:
Finding Millennials

By now, you are hopefully starting to understand who we are and why we act the way we do. In this chapter, we'll transform that knowledge into practical strategies. We'll introduce a step-by-step recruitment plan that we believe will not only help you attract Millennials, but hire better employees, period.

First, let's look at how the Generational Shapes™ influence the way companies recruit. Through their job postings and interview process, companies send messages about their corporate culture that are likely to attract either Boomers, Gen Xers, or Millennials. Companies typically do this without realizing it because they're blind to their own perspective. But when you compare three companies side by side – one triangular, one square, one circular – the differences become crystal clear.

A Tale of Three Shoe Companies

Visit the Careers section of Wolverine Worldwide's website, and you'll see the classically triangular language of the Boomer generation. This shoe company has been building an empire since 1883, amassing several iconic brands, including Keds, Hush Puppies, and Merrell. It has "a mindset focused on growth," and its "footprint can be found in approximately 200 countries and territories throughout the world."

The corporation is looking for employees who want to climb the company pyramid: "We seek out the most talented individuals in our industry, attracting those with a passion for what they do and a desire to achieve great things." They talk about commitment, dedication and achievement. Their internships are "exclusive" and designed to identify individuals for "professional growth" within the company. Their job search engine is organized on a map, geared toward people who want to stay in one location and build a vertical career. Even the title of the page – "Careers" – evokes long-term commitment, as opposed to "Jobs" or "Work With Us," which have a whiff of impermanence.

We're not saying anything is wrong with this language. Wolverine Worldwide may be very effective at recruiting triangular-thinking Baby Boomers and older Gen Xers. If they want to lure Millennials, however, they'll have to reshape their strategy.

Now let's look at Nine West. The stylish shoe company's "Careers" page fits squarely within Gen Xers' square-shaped mindset, a hybrid of triangular and circular perspectives. The text describes the company as "a global leader with a presence in over 78 countries" that offers "limitless opportunities for passionate and creative people to build careers." On the other hand, the introductory video is hip, fun, and individualistic: "You can be anything you want in here," one employee says. The centerpiece "Day in the Life" section puts the focus on consistent schedules and work-life balance. But the tongue-in-cheek tone shows the company doesn't take itself too seriously. And spotlighting employees and their workdays adds a personal touch. However, there's no mention of mission or purpose – values that appeal to the Millennial generation.

Contrast that with a company whose recruitment message is circular to its core: TOMS shoes. The company's One for One® model – buy a product, and they'll provide shoes, water, health care, and bullying prevention programs to people in need –

connects people across the globe in the spirit of giving. In its Jobs section (yes, "Jobs"), TOMS makes it clear they're not building an empire; they're creating a community: "The close-knit culture lets employees feel at home with one another, making for a supportive, collaborative and authentic atmosphere." They talk about the "TOMS family" and "tribe."

TOMS' message caters to people interested in "creating meaningful experiences," not in collecting possessions. They highlight work-life blend, not work-life balance: Their headquarters, close to the beach, features "an open, collaborative atmosphere inside and plenty of workspace outside to take advantage of the nice weather."

The company's internships are geared toward budding entrepreneurs who want to expand their careers laterally, not vertically: "We're confident that by the time you finish the 10-week [internship], you'll be fully equipped to start your own socially conscious business." Their language evokes circular dinner table conversations: "TOMS interns have the opportunity to add real value to the company. To have a voice and be heard. To have an opinion that matters." Their socially conscious message engages people who want to change the world: "Work with us to help improve lives." "Make a difference in your life and someone else's."

TOMS' site is so perfectly calibrated to the Millennial mindset, it's clear they are purposely targeting our generation. And they're doing a great job.

In these examples, we're just looking at the messages corporations send on the jobs page of their websites. But businesses do so much more that influences the demographic and caliber of employees they attract. Let's zoom in on each step of the recruitment process – before, during and after the interview – to show you how to turn your company into a magnet for the best Millennials.

Before the Interview: A Circular Design

Long before HR posts an ad on a jobs website, every employee in your company can participate in "passive recruiting." The term sounds lazy, but it isn't. It's a *Field of Dreams* strategy:

If you build a company that Millennials love, they'll come to you. They'll come to you as customers, as clients, and as candidates. How can you create the company of Millennials' dreams? Here are four steps you can take.

1. Make products and offer services Millennials love to use. It's not rocket science; it's neuroscience. If we're spending our days Googling things on our Samsung or Apple phone while wearing Nike shoes and standing in line at Starbucks, we're going to think of those companies first when we consider where we want to work. And, in fact, those companies are all in the top 20 favorite brands of Millennials, according to a 2016 survey from ad agency Moosylvania.

Obviously, there's no magic formula for becoming a wildly popular brand. But if what you create is user-friendly, readily available, cool, inexpensive, and fits within the lifestyle of our tech-savvy, convenience-obsessed, constantly busy, caffeinated generation, you'll have a better shot at gaining a Millennial fandom.

2. Align your company with Millennial values. Let's be clear: Companies should be ethical and socially conscious because it's the right thing to do, not because it may lure customers. But being a good company – in all senses of that word – also makes sound business sense.

Millennials want to work with businesses that make the world a better place. For example, Chipotle sources its meat from humanely-focused farms, and Levi's launched a strategy to save billions of gallons of water in its manufacturing process. American Eagle and Dove both stopped Photoshopping their models and started featuring "real" women of diverse races and sizes. These environmentally friendly, body-positive, pro-diversity messages resonate with our generation. It's no accident all those companies are in Millennials' top 60 favorite brands, according to the Moosylvania survey.

3. Treat your employees well. Again, this is the right thing to do – and it's also the smart thing to do. Both customers and potential employees are impressed by businesses that follow the Golden Rule. Starbucks has gone a long way toward wooing Millennials (and people of all generations) by offering health insurance to its part-time "partners" and by paying its employees' college tuition. No company is more famous for treating its employees well than Google, which offers "Googlers" three organic meals a day, free fitness classes, the freedom to work on personal projects part of the time, and a multitude of other perks.

Motivated, happy employees work harder (and smarter), stay with your company longer, and are fantastic ambassadors for your business. Which brings us to the next step...

4. Tell the world about the good you do. You can accomplish this through clever social media campaigns, press releases, advertising, and by sponsoring charities aligned with your ethics. You can also do this through your employees. Enthusiastic employees tell their friends, clients, and social media followers about how great your company is. Though they'll do this naturally, you should also give them a social media plan and train them to promote specific messages about the company's mission and brand. Today's Twitter followers could be tomorrow's employees.

As the word spreads, Millennials will seek out and research your company. It's essential that your website spotlights the cultural qualities that are important to our generation.

As the word spreads, Millennials will seek out and research your company. It's essential that your website spotlights the cultural qualities that are important to our generation. Here's an excellent example of a company highlighting its circular ethos.

Case Study: Rackspace

"Are you a Racker?" asks this Texas-based cloud computing company on its jobs page. The question is strategic. Immediately, you're invited to ask whether your identity matches the company's. This engages Millennials, who see our jobs as who we are – extensions of our personalities.

Click on the link, and you're introduced to "the Rackspace family," featuring descriptions of employees' personalities in big red boxes: "a cloud enthusiast with a heart for service," "committed to learning, growing and innovating," "dedicated to making a positive impact." Each employee is spotlighted in a video, and they don't talk about how they fill their schedules. They talk about relationships and character: "Rackers can bring their true, authentic self to work." "We really lean on each other, for knowledge, for mentorship. When we find tribal knowledge, we crush it." "We talk more about what people do well than what they don't do well." Below each video and personality description, in tiny pale print, is the individual's job title. Why is that significant? Because it makes a clear statement: *Who you are is more important than the position you hold. This company is not comprised of ranks you step into as you climb a pyramid; it's made up of unique individuals who are valued members of a family.* That's the essence of a circular household, and it's the essence of a circular business.

In a video titled "Once a Racker, Always a Racker," former employees discuss how their experience at Rackspace helped them create a new company. Can you imagine a competitive, triangular corporation showing off interviews with people who quit? But a circular company is like a family. In a family, you learn from each other, you contribute, and eventually, you leave the nest. But you always stay connected.

Millennials grew up in circular families. They want to continue to grow in circular businesses, like this one.

Active Recruiting

You're starting to see what a circular company looks like (we'll go into more detail in the next chapters). You know how to build a reputation as a business Millennials will love, and how to generate buzz about your company. Now let's walk through the process of transforming your recruiting plan from triangular to circular.

When people are hired in a triangular system, the bosses at the top of the pyramid are often unaware who's being hired because they're too high up to be bothered, while the people at the bottom are deemed too low to be informed. HR often operates in a silo. Many managers never see the job ads that attract people who eventually report to them. It's not uncommon for employees to bump into a new hire at the water cooler and have no idea who they are, even though they'll be expected to work together on the next project.

There are legitimate reasons for structuring a system this way. A director who's busy managing a team shouldn't be tasked with wading through hundreds of resumes. However, when a system is too compartmentalized and hierarchical, it can result in surprises and poor decisions. If a new hire clashes with coworkers and the company culture, or quits because their expectations didn't match their work reality, it wastes everybody's time (and money).

A circular structure can help solve those issues. Here's how to reshape your recruitment plan:

Explain to your employees how your company hires and what you're looking for in new recruits. You can communicate this through a video, infographic, emails, meetings or whatever method fits your culture.

Involve your employees in recruiting. Tell them how they should spread the word – through social media and other methods – that the company is hiring. Inform them where questions and applications should be directed. Maybe HR could write various Tweets, Facebook posts, Reddit messages, etc. publicizing the job opening. Employees could pick from those and send them to their followers and friends.

Before writing the job description, discuss the position with employees who do this job (or a similar job) and those who'll be working with the new hire. Your staff can give you a better idea of the qualifications you should mention, and it will further involve your coworkers in the hiring process.

By taking a communal approach to recruiting, you're sending the message that it's not just HR's responsibility to find good candidates; it's everyone's responsibility. Your employees will feel valued and invested in growing the team. Plus, it's a good way to get feedback on employee morale. You can get a read on how enthusiastic (or not) employees are about inviting their friends and followers to join them at the company.

Find Millennials where we are. Millennials search for jobs in many of the same places other generations do – general sites like LinkedIn, plus industry-specific outlets like AngelList (for startups) and Mediabistro (for media jobs).

But far more than other generations, we look for jobs on social media. According to Glassdoor, 79 percent of job seekers scan social media for openings. Millennials follow the brands we like on Twitter, Facebook and Instagram. So sending out a notice on your company's social media channels targets an audience that's already attracted to your company. Many of us belong to Facebook groups specific to our work (some private, some public) and participate in Reddit conversations related to our fields. Seek out these platforms, and you'll be able to publicize job openings to a motivated, proactive audience with specialized skills.

Look for "I will" rather than IQ. The qualities hiring managers looked for in 1967 are not necessarily the qualities they should look for in 2017. In the days when file cabinets ruled and computers were the size of a room, an employee's accumulated knowledge was priceless. The people who knew the most – who had the highest "IQ" – rose higher and faster in the ranks. Now, information is cheap. In many fields, everyone has access to accumulated knowledge. So when you're hiring Millennials, the differentiating factor is often not their IQ. More often, it's their "I will" – their motivation, enthusiasm, grit, and perseverance to accomplish the work.

Obviously, every field requires different skills and qualities. Enthusiasm and grit alone can't make one a great neurosurgeon or a great novelist. So you'll have to determine what blend of "I will" and "IQ" you're looking for with each position.

(Re)consider the job title. Some companies feel they need to catch Millennials' attention with hip job titles like Code Ninja

or Captain of Buzz. But no one looking for a job is going to put "Trend Jedi" into a search engine. A hip job title will make it difficult for job seekers to find your posting. Conversely, if recruiters are searching LinkedIn for a marketing executive, they're not going to find the person who has "Brand Evangelist" on their resume. When it comes to job postings, stick to classic titles.

Write a circular job description. Think back to the three shoe companies at the beginning of this chapter. A triangular job description is going to attract triangular thinkers. To attract Millennials, emphasize the circular values that are important to us. Here's what we mean:

A triangular description talks about the history of the company and what it does: "For 45 years, Company X has built a reputation for quality across an expanding number of top brands..."

A circular description states the mission of the company and why it does what it does: "Company Y wants to see a world where...". "At Company Y, our goal is to...". This will attract Millennials who share your beliefs and are excited about helping your company realize its mission.

A triangular description itemizes a yawn-inducing list of duties and explains where the position fits in the company's hierarchy: "This position will oversee the design process, maintaining the standards of Company X while balancing the needs of the business. The position will report to the director while managing a team of..."

A circular description tells applicants why this job matters.

It also treats them like people, not position titles. For example:

"In this role, you will design a product that inspires and engages our customers to..."

"You will rewrite the software that will enable Company Y to change the way people..."

"You will support our clients in their efforts to..."

A triangular description focuses on an applicant's past experience and "IQ." It assumes that putting in time automatically translates into developing skills:

"Qualifications: 8+ years' experience in sales"

"knowledge of human resources best practices"

"master's degree in relevant field"

"prior experience with X analytics system."

A circular description focuses on the skills and "I will" necessary to deliver results. This is difficult because "I will" isn't quantifiable. It's also hard to determine in a traditional resume and cover letter if an applicant is giving you lip service or genuinely has what it takes.

So what can you do? We offer a seemingly outrageous proposal...

Ditch the resume. Think about the times you've applied for jobs. Did you feel your resume really showcased your unique skills and talents? Chances are, the answer is "No." You can probably think of a time when you worked with someone who did a terrible job with a bad attitude, and you constantly had to pick up their slack. But because you worked at the same company for a similar number of years and did similar tasks, your resume and Mr. Incompetent's resume look basically the same. That's not a system that works for anybody, except for Mr. Incompetent.

The resume is a holdout from triangular times. It's triangular in its very nature: The base, at the bottom, is where you started – your education and first job. Then it builds up, like a ladder of words, to your current position. Writing a skills-based resume as opposed to a position-based resume does a somewhat better job of highlighting abilities. But there's an even better way for applicants to prove they have the skills, and for hiring managers to determine if candidates have the "I will."

 Instead of asking for a resume, ask candidates to complete job-relevant tasks.

Instead of asking for a resume, ask candidates to complete job-relevant tasks. For example, if you're hiring a PR or marketing person, ask them to write a press release or create a flier publicizing an event. If you're in a service industry, give applicants specific scenarios and ask them how they would solve the problems. Think about the requirements of the position. Will they need to make a video? Pitch ideas? Write code? Ask them to do that in the application. Get creative. One company, posting a coding job on Reddit, required applicants to solve a tricky coding riddle just to know what email address to send their application to.

This method of recruiting requires careful consideration. It would be unreasonable to ask applicants to embark on an extremely time-consuming project. And it would be unethical to use the application process to get work projects done for free, or to steal applicants' ideas. So it's essential to design tasks that are appropriate, fair, and revealing. If done thoughtfully, this can be an excellent way to find people who take initiative, work hard, really want to be part of your company, and truly have the skills and grit it takes to deliver on the job.

During the Interview: A Circular Approach

Before we reimagine the interview, think back to a typical interview you had with a traditional organization. Most likely, you were sequestered in a room with one to three people and asked triangular questions: "Where do you see yourself in five years?" "What can you offer Company X that other applicants can't?" "Tell me about an accomplishment you are most proud of." You prepared for these types of questions and, although you told the truth, you essentially gave them the answers they wanted to hear. You probably didn't get much of a feel for the office's culture or the people in various departments you'd be working with. And the people interviewing you didn't get a real sense for how you'd behave on the job or how you'd fit into the larger culture.

The circular approach remedies some of these shortcomings, and is more Millennial-friendly. Let's go through the steps.

Conduct the interview in a relevant place. Choose a setting that's closest to the one where the new hire will be working. This will give the candidate a good sense of the atmosphere and culture they can expect. Plus, it gives you an opportunity to see how the candidate fits into that atmosphere. It's in nobody's best interest to interview an applicant in your chic, hushed headquarters if they'll actually be working in a noisy warehouse call center.

If possible, simulate the actual work environment. For example, if the position involves working as part of a small team, consider bringing four or five applicants into the interview at the same time. Give them a problem or task and ask them to come up with a solution together. You can observe their ability to communicate, listen, solve problems, be flexible, and make decisions. You can discover who leads democratically, who dominates the conversation, who takes a back seat, and who takes initiative.

Or take your cue from another business that interviewed for a position requiring exceptional social skills. The company invited 15 applicants to a cocktail party also attended by a few dozen of the staff. After the party, each candidate was interviewed separately. The first interview question was: "Tell us the name of every person you met at the party." This is ingenious for several reasons. The setup allowed the company's employees to feel involved in the process and provide vital feedback about how applicants behave in a realistic setting. Then the interviews revealed if the candidates cared enough about building relationships to remember the employees by name.

Give candidates a feel for your culture, while observing how they fit into that culture. Take interviewees around the office and introduce them to your coworkers. Invite employees from various departments to ask the applicants questions. Give applicants a task that simulates what they'd be doing on the job. For example, if you're at a magazine, have them pitch story ideas and provide feedback on cover options. If you're at a software company, sit down with them and have them write code. If they'll need to teach people how to do certain tasks, ask them to teach you.

Communicate your company's mission, vision, and values. Talk about how your company helps the world and how this position will further that mission.

Clearly and honestly explain the responsibilities of the position. Many hiring managers feel they need to win Millennials over by glamorizing the perks and making the office sound like a playground. Savvy Millennials will see through this, while less experienced ones will only be set up for disappointment and may quit when they realize the truth. Spotlight what makes your company great, but also be realistic about the tedious and challenging aspects of the job. You're looking for someone who wants the job, not the perks.

Share your company's social media policy. Does your office ban social media usage during work hours? Millennials want to know that.

Ask circular interview questions focused on skills and "I will." Here are a few examples:

- Describe an idea or project you originated. How did you

determine whether the idea could work? How did you communicate your plan to others? How did you implement it?

- What do you like best about working with a team? What qualities do you bring to a team?

- How can you contribute to our company's mission?

- Tell me about a time at a previous job when you recognized something that could be improved and took steps to solve it without being asked.

- Describe your process when you're assigned a job-appropriate task.

- What types of work do you like doing best, and why?

- What work do you always try to avoid, and why?

- What have you done to make your work more efficient? Effective? Rewarding?

- What do you do differently than other people in your occupation?

- How do you like to receive feedback?

After the Interview: Circular Hiring

Congratulations. You've found the best applicant for the position. Now what? In a triangular system, the hiring manager gives the successful applicant a call and tells them to show up for training next Monday. Circular hiring is more personal, communal, and fun.

Instead of just phoning, give the new hire a box with their favorite candy and items relating to their interests and personality. Or make a short video of employees congratulating the successful applicant and making them feel welcome even before their first day. Send out a message to everyone in the office, or post on your company's social media. Let the world know your team is growing, and introduce your followers to your new hires.

When your new hires arrive, welcome them with company swag, customized t-shirts, or a handwritten note. (Yes, even tech-native Millennials value a handwritten letter from the boss.)

Instead of plunking a big, boring company handbook onto their desk and telling them to read it, make learning the ropes fun. Consider turning it into an interactive game: Give new hires a "passport" and have them go around to all the departments, meeting people and learning what they do. At each department, they can get their passport stamped or signed. Once they've completed it, they can get a prize like a gift certificate.

After experiencing your company's circular recruitment process, your new hires will feel like valued members of your company. They'll be motivated by your mission and understand how they can contribute to that mission.

They'll be off to a great start – and so will you. In the next chapter, we'll show you how you can build on that momentum and keep your employees excited about working for your company.

Real-World Story: Millennial Perspective
Jonathan Roger, Operations Director at AndPlus

*"One of the questions I always try to ask is,
'Is there anything you want to learn?'"*

Jonathan (JD) Roger has come a long way since he found his job on a Reddit thread. As Operations Director of custom software company AndPlus, he oversees the company's entire open portfolio, including allocations, operations, and processes. What makes AndPlus fascinating is that it's a company with practically zero turnover. It's also a diverse business that employs Boomers, Gen Xers, and lots of Millennials, including Roger.

How does the company attract top Millennial talent, plus maintain such a high retention rate across generations? Here's Roger's perspective:

FIRST, RECRUIT TALENT, NOT TITLES: "One thing I make clear to our recruiters is that we're not looking for specific seniority levels," Roger says. "We're really looking for talented people, regardless of age or experience or anything like that – talented people who can write their code for an engineer and who we can bring into our process, rather than just trying to get somebody with a lot of experience. When I'm looking for somebody, I'm looking to tell them, 'We know that you may be a junior resource, but you're somebody who we think has a lot of talent, who we think can rise quickly.' I'm always looking for opportunities to give people more of a leadership role."

SECOND, LOOK FOR DEPTH AND ABILITY IN THE INTERVIEW:
"We'll ask them questions about what they've worked with before,"
Roger explains. "And we found that helps weed out some people… If
they can't talk with a satisfactory depth about what they've done before,
then we know they're not talented. Then, for engineering, we do live
coding exercises where we have them write code with us and in front
of us. And we found that the people we hired who are real talents don't
have a problem doing that."

THIRD, HIGHLIGHT THE COMPANY'S CULTURE AND BENEFITS:
"In interviews, we really do try to highlight that we've got a lot of people
who have been here five, six, seven years. Our attrition rate is basically
zero. The only people who have left have gone because of a change in
their life circumstance. Nobody's really left because they were unhappy
here. So I think highlighting our culture is really important. I try to point
out some of the benefits we have here. We have a gym in our office. We
get catered lunches on Fridays. We have flexible working hours. We get
a lot of holidays and a lot of time off. A lot of places, they're doing beer
on tap at work, and a work happy hour. I think having a variety of cool
things in your office is important to Millennials."

FOURTH, PERSONALIZE MOTIVATION AND INCENTIVES: "I think
Millennials are looking for individualized motivational efforts. I think
everybody's got a different driver. And I think the Millennial generation
is really where management is starting to learn that. So one guy may not
be motivated by getting an extra couple hundred bucks in his paycheck.
He may be motivated by, 'Hey, let's give him an extra day off or let's send
him to a Red Sox game.' Knowing your employees and individualizing
your motivators for them is important."

FIFTH, GIVE MILLENNIALS OPPORTUNITIES FOR GROWTH: "We tell people here that we're always looking for an opportunity to let you advance in your career. We will allow you to advance as fast as you're able and as fast as we're able to let you. So I think giving them ample opportunities to prove themselves and to let them move up is a big deal for people in my generation." That could mean lateral advancement as much as vertical advancement, Roger says. "We encourage our people to learn new languages and new platforms. I try to have one-on-ones every other month with all my engineers and team members. And one of the questions I always try to ask is, 'Is there anything you want to learn?' And I had somebody who works on the Android coming in to tell me, 'Hey, I'd really like to learn how they write iOS apps.' I told her, 'As soon as I get a chance, I'll let you start getting into that.'"

TAKEAWAY QUESTIONS:

- Are you prioritizing ability and "I will" in your recruiting process, as opposed to years of experience?
- Do you know what motivates each individual on your team, and are you personalizing their incentives?
- Are you asking your staff, "Is there anything you want to learn?"

CHAPTER 3

•

Retaining:
Keeping Millennials

We've all heard the stereotypes and seen the splashy headlines: "Millennials: The Job-Hopping Generation." "Gen Y can't commit to anything." "Millennials aren't loyal to companies like previous generations were. It's because they're so entitled." But is that really true?

Disregard Stereotypes

The Bureau of Labor Statistics (BLS) paints a different picture. According to a longitudinal study of nearly 10,000 people, the average latter-year Baby Boomer (those born between 1957 and 1964) held 11.7 jobs between ages 18 and 48. That means they job-hopped an average of every 2.5 years – about the same rate as Millennials. Of course, most of that job-switching happened when the Boomers were younger. Now that they're in their 50s, they've settled into their current positions for a longer period of time, according to BLS statistics from 2016:

Employee age and average length of tenure with their current employer:
   55 to 64: 10.1 years
   45 to 54: 7.9 years
   35 to 44: 4.9 years
   25 to 34: 2.8 years

So maybe job-hopping is a trait of the young rather than of Millennials in particular. We won't know for sure until Millennials turn 55 and statisticians can compare us side by side with Boomers. In the meantime, it's smart to view generational stereotypes with skepticism – especially in the era of clickbait.

In the spring of 2016, several prominent news outlets including CNN published provocative articles about those chronically job-jumping Millennials. The impetus was a LinkedIn study that made this bold claim: "Over the last 20 years, the number of companies people worked for in the five years after they graduated [college] has nearly doubled." LinkedIn then goes into the details: "People who graduated between 1986 and 1990 averaged more than 1.6 jobs, and people who graduated between 2006 and 2010 averaged nearly 2.85 jobs."

Wait, that's a difference of only one job. So, Millennials who graduated during the Great Recession held one more job in five years than Gen Xers who graduated during a time of relative prosperity? That's so unsurprising it's yawn-worthy. But when journalists spin it to play into our stereotypes of "kids these days," it strengthens our biases.

And what about the idea that Millennials are disloyal, whereas previous generations stayed in their jobs due to a sense of loyalty? Well, that would mean older generations were saying to themselves, "I don't like working at this company, but they've been good to me, so I'll stay." Isn't it more common that people felt they had to stay because the salary was good and the mortgage needed to be paid? Or that they wanted to live in the town where they had friends and family, and there weren't many other options? Or that they'd get a pension if they stayed? Or that changing jobs seemed daunting and uncertain, so they put it off, and the years slipped by?

All those reasons are based on practicality and security, not necessarily loyalty. Millennials have an inherent sense of practicality. We saw our Boomer parents stay for years in jobs that made them unhappy, and then they got laid off anyway. That's why we prioritize fulfillment over job security.

> *It's not true that we're a bunch of disloyal, entitled commitment-phobes. But it is true that keeping us in a job is more challenging than it was with previous generations.*

It's not true that we're a bunch of disloyal, entitled commitment-phobes. But it is true that keeping us in a job is more challenging than it was with previous generations. That's because we're motivated by much more than a paycheck and benefits. We need to be motivated by a cause we believe in, a collaborative and flexible culture we can thrive in, and opportunities to contribute and be challenged – from day one.

In this chapter, we'll show you how to shift your motivational perspective from triangular to circular. You'll master the practical steps to retain Millennials. And you'll see how those practices will help improve your business as a whole. Because it's not just Millennials driving changes in today's office, the very nature of work itself is changing.

Motivation: Shift from Compensation to Cause

Scroll through recent articles and books on how to retain employees, and you'll see a lot of attention devoted to traditional triangular "carrots": "Provide a competitive benefits package including health insurance, life insurance, and a 401(k) plan," the experts say. "Employees should be rewarded with raises, annual bonuses, and immediate cash payments to motivate high performance."

Millennials need to pay bills like everyone else. But remember that what keeps them working at a company and going the extra mile every day, is not just the paycheck. Six in 10 Millennials say their current employer's "sense of purpose" is part of the reason they chose to work there, according to a 2015 Deloitte survey. If us Millennials are emotionally invested in a company's mission – and believe we're directly contributing to that mission – we're in. We'll be excited to work for the company, and we'll give it our all.

But it's not just Millennials who have a different motivational model. Economists and scientists say that, because of the changing nature of work, the motivational model based totally on money is outdated. In the modern American marketplace, almost everyone needs to be motivated by a mission and their own inner drive.

In his 2011 book *Drive*, Daniel H. Pink describes the tectonic shifts shaking the bedrock of motivation theory. During much of the 1900s, the thinking went something like this: "Work consists mainly of simple, not particularly interesting tasks. The only way to get people to do them is to incentivize them properly and monitor them carefully." That quote is from management consultant Frederick Winslow Taylor, and for many decades, he was right. Both blue and white collar work were largely formulaic and routine – think assembly line workers and file clerks. Employees were motivated to perform these tasks strictly by their financial compensation. This jibed with their triangular mindset: Work is for a paycheck, not for fulfillment.

Then something shifted. Many of those formulaic jobs were replaced by technology or sent overseas. Now, the vast majority of work is complex, often requiring high-level decision-making and creative problem-solving. Almost 70 percent of the U.S. job growth occurs in professions that require this kind of complex thinking, according to a study from the consulting firm McKinsey & Co.

To perform these jobs well, you can't be motivated purely by traditional, triangular carrots and sticks. Numerous scientific studies show that focusing on financial compensation actually thwarts creative problem-solving. Whereas passion, purpose, and striving for personal accomplishment stimulates creative thinking.

Think about it. If you don't care about your mission and you're just putting in time for a paycheck, you can still be an efficient file clerk, but you'd probably make a terrible social media manager, software developer, speech-language pathologist, or environmental engineer.

WAYS TO SHIFT MOTIVATIONAL FOCUS

Both Millennials and contemporary careers demand a shift in motivational focus from compensation to cause. The following are some steps you can take to facilitate this shift in your own company:

Get clear about your company's mission. Your mission is not a statement of what you do. It's why you do what you do, and how you change the world and people's lives. Here are some real-life examples that would inspire Millennials or idealists in any generation:

Energy company PK Clean envisions a world with zero

landfill waste, where plastics do not destroy the environment but are converted into sustainable fuel.

Toy and app company GoldieBlox empowers young girls to love engineering and build futures in science.

Outdoor retailer Patagonia encourages people to enjoy nature and helps protect the planet's natural resources.

Communicate your mission constantly. Talk about it during recruiting, at meetings, with clients, and anytime you need to make a major decision. Keep the mission at the forefront of your employees' minds.

Share the results of your mission. Think of various ways to share with employees how your mission is succeeding. For example, medical device company Stryker encourages staffers to meet patients, join sales reps as they visit customers, and observe surgeries. Talking to people who are alive and healthy thanks to the company's products is a powerful motivator, whether you're a Millennial, a Gen Xer, or a Boomer.

Pay a fair wage and don't stop there. Salary is not the 'be all and end all' of motivation. Millennials do care about salary, benefits and raises. We certainly wouldn't recommend that companies pay Millennials – or anyone else – unfair salaries in exchange for the opportunity to work for a good cause. But think of financial compensation in terms of Maslow's Hierarchy of Needs. Security and basic needs must be met before humans can think about self-actualization. In the same way, a fair salary, benefits and raises must exist so employees can focus on the things that really excite them - a cause and a culture they believe in. Speaking of which...

Culture: Shift from Competition to Collaboration

There's a reason the triangular system is often called the Rat Race. It's a competitive structure that pits employees against each other as they scramble up the corporate ladder. From the triangular perspective, this is the only way to spur employees and the company to success.

Millennials, however, are not interested in running this race. Millennials want to work with you, not against you. Nearly nine in 10 of us prefer a collaborative environment rather than a competitive one, according to a study from the Intelligence Group, a New Jersey-based research firm. We think a collaborative structure can be just as conducive to success as a competitive one — maybe even more so, since it avoids pitting employees against each other in a competitive environment. To see what we mean, let's look into the "minds" of two famous corporations.

In 2008, *Scientific American Mind* columnist Michael Shermer wrote a story exploring the psychology of two companies on opposite sides of the competitive-collaborative spectrum. The first, a hyper-hierarchical triangular corporation, operated under the assumption that people are primarily motivated by greed and fear. The company then set up a ruthlessly competitive system that forced its employees to be motivated by greed and fear.

It implemented a Peer Review Committee – nicknamed "Rank and Yank" – that graded employees on a scale of 1 to 5. Those rated 5 were banished to corporate purgatory and given two weeks to find a new position or be kicked out. The entire office knew who was in limbo, since every employee's review and photograph were posted on the internal website. The idea was that employees would be spurred to success by a desire to avoid shame.

Every six months, 10 to 20 percent of the staff was fired. Because rankings were based on numeric comparisons instead of qualitative worth, managers cut deals for numbers: "Do this for me, and I'll give you a 2 instead of a 3." Contrary to expectations, this cut-throat system brought out the worst in its employees. It encouraged the backstabbing, cheating and stealing that led to the spectacular demise of this notorious company: Enron.

The second company utilized a new structure: circular. This company believed that collaboration, rather than competition, would bring out the best in its employees. It operated under the assumption that if people respected and trusted, they will reciprocate in kind. Their employees – many of them Millennials – were given great free perks and loads of autonomy. They reciprocated by working long hours with dedication and creativity.

During weekly meetings, all employees – regardless of position – could ask questions of the founders and other execs about company issues and projects. "We strive to maintain the open culture often associated with startups, in which everyone is a hands-on contributor and feels comfortable sharing ideas and opinions," explains the company's "Our Culture" page. This transparent, cooperative atmosphere encourages a cross-pollination of ideas. It fosters the innovation that has contributed to the spectacular success of this corporation: Google.

Of course, Enron and Google are extreme examples. We're not saying all businesses with competitive structures fail and all cooperative ones triumph. But Google (and companies like it) prove that a circular, collaborative workplace can be incredibly successful in the competitive marketplace. Plus, collaborative businesses are the kind of places where employees – especially Millennials – want to stay.

WAYS TO SHIFT FROM A COMPETITIVE TO A COLLABORATIVE ATMOSPHERE

Encourage open and democratic communication. Creating a collaborative culture does not mean everybody has to waste time in endless meetings dominated by groupthink. Occasional face-to-face meetings are necessary. But you can absolutely foster cooperation in an office where people largely work independently and even remotely. The key is to create a transparent environment where everyone is encouraged to share ideas and no one is stymied by status or bureaucracy.

During Google's regular "all-hands" meetings, for example, all Googlers can ask questions and pitch ideas directly to founders Larry Page and Sergey Brin. At the strategic consulting firm Accenture, CEO Julie Sweet banned the corporate memo – a hierarchical holdout that resembles a formal decree issued by an unseen monarch. Instead, Sweet live-streams informal video messages and employees can instantly send her questions online. Other businesses, such as Slack, use intra-office communication technology to promote an "all hands on deck" spirit so everyone can generate and weigh in on ideas.

Recognize individual contributions. Even when the emphasis is on the team, individuals must be given credit for their contributions, publicly and privately. Millennials recognized for their contributions are more inclined to keep bringing ideas to the table. But employees who feel their input is not valued, or that other people are stealing their credit, will stop speaking up and eventually leave.

Focus on people's strengths, not their weaknesses. At Rackspace, newcomers take a StrengthsFinder assessment so that their managers can assign tasks and provide opportunities best suited to those strengths. This way, employees are valued for what they uniquely do best, not stymied by what they can't do well.

Implement a mentoring program. Mentoring encourages employees to learn from each other and not compete against each other. This is especially true of non-traditional mentoring programs such as peer mentoring or reverse mentoring, in which Millennials mentor more seasoned employees. (Learn more about Millennial-friendly mentoring programs in Chapter 4.)

Career Goals: Shift from the Corporate Ladder to a Seat at the Table

In triangular companies, new employees are expected to watch what they say and do, and "pay their dues." Motivated by a desire to have their voices heard, they slowly step up the corporate ladder. Once they arrive on the top rung, they often find that power doesn't bring freedom but rather a whole new set of constraints and responsibilities. Having spent so long climbing their way up, they still feel pressure to censor what they say and not rock the boat. In this way, triangular systems encourage staid, risk adverse thinking. They can create companies that are as slow to adapt to change as the Titanic was to steer around icebergs.

Today's world is changing faster than ever. As a result, companies have to be more adaptable and innovative than ever. This means companies need to hear all the voices at the table – right now.

Today's world is changing faster than ever. As a result, companies have to be more adaptable and innovative than ever. This means companies need to hear all the voices at the table – right now. There can be a whole lot of resistance to that notion, particularly when it comes to Millennials.

While growing up, many Millennials were encouraged to speak up at the dinner table, share opinions, and teach their parents about technology. In the workplace, they expect a similar seat at the table. Because we grew up witnessing the explosion of Facebook, Twitter, and other tech giants – all sparked and fueled by an employee-driven entrepreneurial spirit – we want to influence our companies in this way, too (including those of us who work outside of Silicon Valley).

This desire to speak up often gets misunderstood as entitlement and people assume we want to be treated like the CEO from day one. But that's not true. We do respect experienced leaders (when they're respectable). We acknowledge that we don't yet have the same experience, but that shouldn't stop us from bringing good ideas to the table. Because we want our voices to be heard from day one, and don't care about stepping up the corporate ladder, it's essential you create an environment that encourages open communication and transparency. And it becomes a win-win. Millennials become creative contributors and organizations become innovators.

WAYS TO SHIFT FROM THE VERTICAL LADDER TO THE HORIZONTAL

Give Millennials a voice. This can be as simple as being open to ideas from all employees and implementing practices we discussed in the collaboration section. But you can do even more. Many leading organizations are implementing "360 degree reviews" that give Millennials and other workers the opportunity to evaluate the boss – a concept that was unheard of in the Boomers' generation and not common for Gen Xers. Some businesses are conducting "stay" interviews in addition to traditional exit interviews. Instead of waiting until an employee leaves to find out what the company might do to improve, managers are talking with employees about why they are staying and what suggestions they have.

Of course, considering employees' ideas can be time consuming and present challenges. Millennials are often brimming with so many ideas that it can be difficult to track and identify the really great ones. In brainstorming sessions, Millennials often throw out ideas that get discounted simply because no one has any solid information to go on. This can leave them feeling disheartened and discouraged. And potentially good ideas can get left on the table.

Instead, encourage your Millennial employees to write down all their ideas and conduct research on the one they deem most worthy. Have them list the pros and cons of their idea with a potential plan for implementing it. This way you can provide more focused and constructive feedback, and they'll feel like you're giving their input respect and real consideration.

Allow Millennials (and other employees) to chart their own paths. Millennials care more about forging a career path than following a traditional, prescribed path for success. In response to this, innovative businesses are allowing Millennials and others to work with their managers to create custom career paths, complete with goals and objectives. The Fennemore Craig law firm, for example, has implemented personal development plans for every associate (non-partner) attorney.

It might seem like letting someone blaze their own trail is merely catering to an individual's whims. But when done carefully, it enables employees to maximize their potential, which benefits the company. These employees, satisfied that they're working in their element, are more likely to stay, which obviously reduces the cost of turnover. In addition, these plans help the company to be more flexible in taking on new projects or expanding into new areas, since current employees can more easily take on different tasks that align with their strengths.

Have regular talks with employees about their professional goals and passions. What attracts people to a job isn't necessarily what keeps them in the job. As their skills develop and they take on new tasks, and as the company evolves, their interests and goals often change. So it's important that employees and managers are on the same page about potential new directions. It often happens that employees seek an opportunity at another company because they are unaware that a similar position might exist or be created at their current company.

During these career planning sessions, also encourage employees to set goals that incorporate work-life blend. This sends a message that the company cares about them and wants them to be happy about their work and their life outside the office.

Give Millennials training and abundant opportunities to grow. Decades ago, training was *de rigueur* at companies since it was assumed employees would stay for years. Now it's often assumed that training is wasted on employees, particularly Millennials, since they'll probably leave in a year or two. But this sends the message that your company doesn't value Millennials or believe they'll stick around. And that's the reason they don't. It creates a self-fulfilling prophecy.

Training can come in many forms. To help retain Millennials, Quicken Loans gives full-time employees an average of 350 hours of training every year. Amazon offers a month-long training and leadership program for new hires, while the company's "Virtual Contact Center" trains employees to work remotely. At Location Labs, a mobile security company with a 95 percent retention rate, employees are always recommending the latest management books to each other, and the company will reimburse them for work-related books.

Foster an atmosphere of learning and improvement in your office. Allow Millennials to pursue development opportunities such as attending conferences or leadership workshops. Or take time to participate in professional development webinars or listen to industry-specific podcasts.

"I think giving Millennials opportunities is actually a great motivator," says Jonathan Roger, Operations Director at AndPlus, a custom software development company. "A lot of my Millennial friends get fed up waiting for somebody to leave the company, retire, or get promoted in order to advance. They don't feel like they'll ever have that opportunity to get more responsibility because people from a previous generation are occupying that space and there's no room for them to grow, so they leave. The friends I've had who have consistently been given more opportunities, more responsibilities, whether lateral or vertical, have been the ones who've stayed at their jobs. That's why I'm really enjoying what I do now, because I feel like every day, I get a new responsibility. And that's always a pretty awesome perk."

Coach rather than manage. Coaching – a circular approach – is about motivating Millennials to allow them to exercise leadership skills and let their entrepreneurial spirits shine. Managing, on the other hand, is a triangular, top-down approach, that often dictates how employees work. This approach tends to make people reluctant, or even afraid, to share ideas or ask questions. However, as a coach, you can provide employees the tools to succeed and be available to help them, but also give them the space they need to succeed or fail on their own. (Read more about coaching and motivating in Chapter 4.)

Incentives and Feedback: Shift from Annual to Incremental

There is nothing to say about annual reviews except that you'd be hard-pressed to find anyone who sings praises of this triangular tradition. Even by saying it's outdated implies that there was a time when it worked. The very concept of an annual review is baffling because if an employee is doing something badly, why wait 12 months to tell them? Or in the case of exceptional work, where you're trying to reinforce that great performance, you need to give that positive feedback immediately.

That same thinking applies to annual bonuses. Bonuses are often tied to corporate goals, so that can make them impersonal and difficult for employees to understand their individual contribution in achieving them. Plus, the timing means they're not particularly useful as a motivator or reinforcement of positive behavior.

Millennials, because they grew up in an age of instant gratification, are less patient than previous generations, and that presents a problem with the system of annual rewards and feedback.

Millennials, because they grew up in an age of instant gratification, are less patient than previous generations, and that presents a problem with the system of annual rewards and feedback. They don't want to go through an entire year of feeling uncertain and potentially undervalued, so many are prompted to leave. Instead, here are some different steps you can take to reward and give feedback to your Millennial employees.

WAYS TO MOTIVATE AND RETAIN MILLENNIALS WITH INCREMENTAL REWARDS AND FREQUENT FEEDBACK

Provide immediate, specific feedback. We know that it's not easy to shift from the mindset of the annual review to one of frequent feedback unless you think of it like this: You probably already provide frequent feedback in other aspects of your life, which means you understand how valuable this can be. For example, you wouldn't dream of not saying a word for a year after your children misbehaved. Likewise, you wouldn't dream of telling your spouse or significant other that you loved them only on your anniversary. This same logic applies in the workplace. Why present an employee with a performance review in December for work they did in March? That's how ridiculous the annual review seems when you look at it in the real world and from a Millennial perspective.

We instinctively know that people need immediate feedback about improving on a poorly executed task or being complimented for a creating a great product. This instant feedback gives them the confidence to take action, whether it's to fix a problem or to repeat a positive behavior. Bosses are more inclined to give immediate feedback only when an employee is doing something wrong, whereas the simple act of praising someone ends up being relegated to an annual review or when handing out a bonus. (You'll find more detail about motivating Millennials through feedback in Chapter 4.

Offer frequent individualized rewards instead of generic annual incentives. Imagine it's the end of the year and you got your bonus check at the same time as your coworkers. How valued as an individual would that make you feel? Perhaps it's better than nothing but somehow it doesn't feel like it is acknowledging your personal achievements and hard work. Now imagine your boss knows you like to participate in IRONMAN competitions and she informs you that because of your great performance, she's paying for your next IRONMAN competition. How much more valued would you feel?

Or maybe you worked really hard to complete a project, and your boss says, "Fantastic job. I really appreciated your creative approach and that you worked the weekend to get the project done on such short notice. Take tomorrow off and spend time with your daughter." How valued would you feel?

Personalized rewards, large or small, are worth far more in emotional currency than annual rewards of any size. Personalized rewards are also far more likely to keep your employees performing well and wanting to stay at your company.

Tailor benefits and perks to Millennials. Offering thoughtful, creative benefits calibrated to the Millennial lifestyle shows you care about them as individuals. For example, because Millennials tend to be socially conscious, they love to volunteer and many take part in company-sponsored volunteer programs or paid volunteer time.

The healthcare company Novo Nordisk pays employees for up to 80 hours a year of community volunteer time. At CHG

Healthcare Services, employees annually nominate coworkers who make the biggest difference in the lives of others. In 2016, four winning employees and their guests got an all-expense-paid trip to Kenya to participate in a volunteer project and safari.

Some companies offer tuition reimbursement, but these plans are less applicable to Millennials buried under student loan debt. This most well-educated generation typically averages $29,000 in student debt in the U.S., and that figure is rising.

The average graduate in 2016 owes $37,172. In order to retain Millennials, several major corporations are offering student-loan debt-reimbursement. PricewaterhouseCoopers pays up to $1,200 per year for six years. Aetna matches up to $2,000 per year for full-time employees, capped at a total of $10,000. The downside is that, unlike tuition reimbursement, student loan debt reimbursement is not (yet) tax-free.

Other suggestions for Millennial-friendly perks might be paying for a gym membership or a Netflix account, offering healthy meals or snacks, or hosting a Friday afternoon happy hour with a keg of local craft beer.

It's important to remember that the oldest Millennials are now reaching their mid-30s, and 40 percent have children. Sadly, with the U.S. being the only developed nation without mandated paid parental leave, companies have to take up this initiative. Millennial parents are highly involved with their children, and many companies are responding to that. Employees at Coca-Cola formed a group called "Coca-Cola Millennial Voices" who pressed for a change of the company's leave policies. In 2017, the company began offering six weeks of paid leave to all new moms and dads, including same-sex couples and adoptive and foster parents. This is in addition to the six to eight weeks of paid leave already provided to birth mothers through short-term disability. Likewise, cloud-based software company Basecamp offers up to six weeks of full-pay maternity and paternity leave. EBay offers up to 12 weeks, and the accounting firm EY (formerly Ernst & Young) offers up to 16 weeks.

If you really want to retain Millennials, remember that nothing matters more to them than quality time – especially with their families.

Schedules: Shift from Work-Life Balance to Work-Life Blend

Millennials often value time and experiences over money, which we discussed in Chapter 1. Because Millennials are digital natives who are used to integrating work and their personal lives, they want to work with companies that provide the flexibility to both work hard and play hard.

WAYS TO PROVIDE THE TOOLS TO ALLOW AN INTEGRATED WORK/ FAMILY LIFE.

Offer flextime and telecommuting. Seventy-five percent of Millennials would like to work remotely some or all of the time, according to the 2016 Deloitte Millennial Survey. In fact, according to a survey from FlexJobs, when Millennials are faced with a really important project, 76 percent prefer to work at home because they find the office too distracting. But it's not just Millennials. Boomers and Gen Xers also want and expect flexible schedules and telecommuting.

Many managers believe that employees working at home will be shirking their responsibilities, but research shows that isn't the case. Stanford University economists randomly selected hundreds of employees at a large Chinese call center to work at home four days a week. Nine months later, the telecommuters were 13 percent more productive. This result ends in the company allowing employees to choose their own schedules and half opted to work remotely. The outcome was a whopping 22 percent boost in productivity.

Outdoor clothing and gear company Patagonia – headquartered in surf-crazy Ventura, California – is famous for giving employees the flexibility to hit the beach when the waves are up. Founder Yvon Chouinard wrote about this policy in his book, *Let My People Go Surfing*. This flexible philosophy doesn't hurt the company, with $600 million in revenue and double-digit annual growth. In addition, they routinely report a single-digit turnover rate. They retain their employees and with good reason.

As you can see by these two examples, telecommuting and flexibility are successful strategies for creating work-life integration. Remember, the key to a successful telecommuting program is to focus on meeting goals within a timeline – not to just fill time. And by giving your employees more latitude to choose when they work and play, the company ultimately wins.

Provide tools for the Millennial work-style. It's not a new secret that job satisfaction (for all generations) hinges on workers having all the tools they need to succeed. Gallup surveys found, more than 20 years ago, that an employer providing the correct workplace tools for success is a key ingredient of employee retention. Fifty years ago, the right tools might have been an office and a personal assistant. Twenty-five years ago, the right tools might have been a personal computer and with a printer at your desk.

Today, the tools needed by a Millennial worker are likely to include: smartphones, tablets, laptops, and high-speed remote virtual private networks that mirror being connected in the office. It's seems to be surprising to Boomer leaders how critical these seemingly small pieces of technology are to Millennials.

Millennials believe that when employers want them to do their best work, they must provide the tools they need to work in virtually anywhere.

Millennial believe that when employers want them to do their best work, they must provide the tools they need to work in virtually anywhere. Millennials will work harder and longer if these tools are available to them.

In the following chapter, you'll see how you can motivate Millennials to do even more and be more efficient.

"Trust your people to own and execute their responsibilities and then have their back as they do it."

If you want to know what Millennials think of triangular versus circular bosses, just ask Christopher Farmer. The Millennial and Category II Manager works in strategic sourcing at Gap Inc., which owns Banana Republic, Old Navy, Athleta, and its namesake brand. During his career at various companies, Farmer has worked with managers on extreme sides of the Generational Shape™ spectrum – and these bosses have affected the staff in very different ways.

Farmer's triangular manager was "very old-school, very command-and-control style," he says. This boss rationed out information like rare coins and enforced a rigid chain of command. "You quickly start to feel like you're an admin man because you're compiling A or analyzing B and sending it back up to him," Farmer explains. "You're just collecting data and putting together reports and sending it up the chain." The effect on the staff was dramatic: Everyone considered moving to a different role in the company or even changing companies.

On the other hand, Farmer's circular boss was "the best boss that I've ever had, hands down." And everyone Farmer worked with agreed. What did this manager do differently? He constantly encouraged his staff to take on new responsibilities, empowered them to take risks, and engaged them with new challenges:

ENCOURAGE: "This boss was always encouraging us to reach beyond our job titles or our job descriptions," Farmer explains. "He would just encourage you to run as fast as you can and take on as much as you felt like you could. And it didn't matter where you found a project, who you were going to work with, what level in the company it was. As long as you were adding value to the company and then challenging yourself to grow and explore new things, he just pushed it, pushed it, pushed it."

EMPOWER: "He would also just trust us to execute it," Farmer says. "And that's a big thing with Millennials. We want to own whatever it is that we are tasked with, and just trust that we'll take care of it. And we're happy – or at least I'm happy – to fall on my face. I'll be the first to admit my mistakes, but I want the opportunity to make those mistakes." Farmer advises other managers to "trust that I'll do what you've tasked me with doing and empower me to do it. Because if I feel like I don't have the power to do what needs to be done, then I start to question what I'm doing there."

ENGAGE: "He and I would have weekly touch-bases, and he would ask, 'Are you bored?'" Farmer says. "And we would talk about things that are encouraging or engaging, and he said, 'Okay. Well, great. But in the future you're going to get bored with this. I know you will. So I'm thinking roughly XYZ for you in the next 6 to 12 to 18 months.' So that's huge for someone like me. Because that means he's looking out for stuff that will really continue to challenge me, and I feel like he has my back. Millennials will do a role for a year and then look for the next role that they can take on. And they aren't always looking for a promotion by moving on. They may be just looking for a different type of challenge, even though it's the same level, same pay, or same compensation package."

"One of the things that I've noticed among people my age or even younger," Farmer adds, "is that we're all very, very curious and we want to understand the way things work – more so than just our limited roles. So in the jobs I've had since I left college, I've been placed with a lot of older generations, and I found that my drive or curiosity actually far exceeds theirs. Or I can explain what our company does or why it's valuable, better than they can, even if they've been at the company for a decade or more. In my observation, the older generation – I'd say middle aged or older than that – they have a tendency to just find a comfortable place and stay there, and kind of just keep their head down, whereas the Millennial tends to always ask, 'What else is there?' or 'What else can I do?'"

TAKEAWAY QUESTIONS:

- What are you doing today to encourage your team to take on new responsibilities that will prepare them for leadership positions in the near future?
- Are you keeping your top Millennials continually engaged with new challenges or asking them periodically if they are bored?
- Are you empowering your team to do more and be more by trusting them to take risks and reach beyond their job descriptions?

CHAPTER 4

•

Realizing:
Motivating and Promoting
Millennials

Now, let's revisit this prediction: by 2030, Millennials will make up 75 percent of the U.S. workforce and will fill most of the leadership roles. It's hard to imagine the 22-year-old you hired recently becoming the CEO of the company, or the director of the department you built from the ground up. But don't forget that the leaders who hired you thought the same thing about you. Just as you looked for the opportunities to prove yourself, so do Millennials.

Unfortunately, 63 percent of Millennials believe their "leadership skills are not being fully developed," according to the 2016 Deloitte Millennial Survey. Just 28 percent of Millennials feel their companies are "making full use of the skills they currently have to offer." This feeling of being underestimated is going to hurt companies – and the economy – in the long run, unless something is done about it soon.

We've now come to the part where you are probably wondering how you can help Millennials realize their full potential. We will show you by introducing some simple formulas that we know will motivate Millennials in solving problems and achieving goals. You'll also see exactly how to provide the type of feedback that helps minimize weaknesses and maximize strengths. We'll explore ways for you to set up Millennial-friendly mentoring programs and show you how to identify potential leaders in a world where the nature of leadership is changing. Finally, we'll talk about how to train Millennials to be motivators, not managers.

Communicating with Millennials

Helping anyone realize their potential starts with effective communication and it's no different with Millennials. Although we've heard of Boomer and Gen X managers being told to shift toward virtual communication (because Millennials prefer technology over in-person meetings), we believe meaningful face-to-face communication is and always will be essential in workplace relationships. Millennials need that personal connection to feel they are being heard. It also helps them to develop the face-to-face communication skills they need to become successful leaders.

COMMUNICATION STRATEGIES TO MOTIVATE MILLENNIALS TO SOLVE PROBLEMS, TAKE OWNERSHIP OF GOALS AND DEVELOP TALENTS

Problem-Solving: The PAR (Problem/Action/Result) Formula

Millennials were born into a fast-paced world. They rattle off messages in 140 characters or less, and are impatient if meetings drift toward pointless digressions or fluffy formalities. They are also very purpose-focused and results-oriented. When communication lacks focus, Millennials feel it wastes their time and dampens their enthusiasm. But a consistent, simple message spurs action.

The PAR Formula is a sure-fire way to structure conversations in a way that ensures getting your point across quickly and clearly. Let's look at each point in the Formula:

Problem: State the problem clearly and concisely, such as, "Sales are down by 15 percent."

Action: Discuss actions that can be taken to resolve the problem. Be sure to involve Millennials in discovering solutions rather than just giving orders. For example, say, "Here are three ways I think we can grow sales. What are some actions you think we could take to grow sales?" This opens Millennials to the opportunity to creatively solve problems, show off their talents, and grow them into leaders – all of which are great motivators.

Result: Highlight the outcome of successfully taking action. But keep in mind that many Boomers make the mistake of talking only about the results the company or the leader gets. For example, saying, "You need to grow sales so the company can reach their $50 million goal" won't motivate Millennials. Instead, the focus should be switched to language that Millennials and their team understands, such as:

- "If you take these actions to grow sales and the company grows, you'll be able to launch that project you want to start."

- "You'll get more volunteer days."

- "Your team will make their bonus goals."

- "You'll have more control over your schedule."

- "We'll be able to devote more resources to the company charity projects you're involved in."

To get it right, PAR must be used in the exact order shown. Like dialing a phone number, PAR is a formula and you cannot switch the order of the letters, just as you cannot switch the numbers when dialing a phone if you want to reach the party you wish to call. This PAR formula must be repeated until the result is achieved because it's easy for employees to get distracted. Consistently focusing on a result is the way to reach it.

Setting Personal Goals: What, Why, and How

The PAR Formula helps motivate Millennials to solve short-term and long-term problems, but a variation is needed for discussing other types of goals. These other types of goals include mapping out an individual career path or launching a personal project. But it's also essential that Millennials take ownership of their goals. For this, you can help them connect with their purpose and passion by asking three questions:

- *What* is your goal?

- *Why* do you want to achieve it?

- *How* can you achieve it?

Here's a real-world example. Jenny Poon is the founder of CO+HOOTS, a Phoenix-based co-working space that is home to about 250 businesses. It's been called the most innovative co-working space in the country, and Poon was named Business Person of the Year 2016 by the *Phoenix Business Journal*. Poon and her staff are all Millennials. Several times a year, she works with them to set goals. She begins by asking them to visualize their goals. "You sit down with them," Poon says, "and say, 'What do you want to accomplish in three months, in six months? Close your eyes. Tell me what you see.' Get down to the nitty gritty of what that goal looks like."

Then she asks why they want to achieve this goal. "One of my mentors once told me to ask the question 'Why?' three to five times, until you really get to the answer of why somebody is doing something," Poon explains. "If they don't truly have a reason, then they're probably not yet ready to take on the leadership role. It needs to be bigger than just, 'I want to make lots of money.'"

Poon says an example of a typical response for CO+HOOTS might be an employee saying, "In a year I want to see 50 different companies hire 50 more people." So, she says, "You ask them why. Why is that important to you? They might say, 'I love meeting all of these people, and I think they deserve to be successful.' Well, why? Where does that come from? Then they start to dig into why this personally matters to them. They might say, 'Because when I was growing up, my parents were entrepreneurs and they failed at their business.' Okay, now it's your life mission to help these people."

"If they can't get down to something that is tied to them personally, they are not truly passionate about it yet," Poon continues. "Every single person on our team has that story that connects them to what they're doing."

Once you've worked through the *what* and the *why*, it's time to move on to the *how*. As a leader, you can guide Millennials as they step back from the big-picture goal and map out the steps necessary to achieve it. The benefit of having Millennials visualize a concrete goal, discover the meaning behind that goal, and outline a step-by-step plan is that "they own that entire process," Poon says. "Everybody wants to feel like they are able to change the world, and once they are able to have a taste of that, it's unstoppable."

Giving Feedback: Timely, Honest, and Actionable

Today's fast-paced economy demands that employees are constantly aware of how they're measuring up so they can quickly change what's not working or repeat the behaviors that are successful. But in most companies, the culture surrounding feedback hasn't caught up with the times.

According to a 2016 Gallup poll, just 19 percent of Millennials receive routine feedback from managers, and only 17 percent believe the feedback they're getting is meaningful.

According to a 2016 Gallup poll, just 19 percent of Millennials receive routine feedback from managers, and only 17 percent believe the feedback they're getting is meaningful.

Actionable feedback that is frequent is essential to engaging Millennials and empowering them to make changes. However, Millennials' desire for feedback often gets framed as "neediness," "insecurity," or "wanting a trophy just for showing up." "I think there is a myth that all Millennials are really self-absorbed and just always looking to be given a trophy for participating," says Jonathan Roger, Operations Director at AndPlus. "I'm not looking for a trophy every time I ask, 'Hey, how'd that go? Do you think that went well?' What I'm really looking for is feedback. I look for feedback from my boss and from my peers every time we go out of a meeting and every time we finish a sprint. I'm looking for people to ask me, 'Is there something I could've done better there?'"

The real reason Millennials want and need constant feedback is because they have always gotten it from their parents and teachers. Boomers and Gen Xers didn't grow up with this frequent feedback, so they developed the thinking that, "As long as nobody's saying anything, I must be doing a good job." Millennials developed the opposite belief, which translates into thinking that, "If nobody's saying anything, I'm not doing a good job."

Millennials thrive on innovating and taking risks, but can't do so if they don't know where they stand. They can't confidently make those leaps without feedback. In a traditional triangular company where employees are expected to follow orders and preserve the status quo, it's not necessary to constantly know how you're measuring up. But if your company is launching new ventures, innovating and changing, you absolutely need constant input. To help Millennials in their quest to grow and improve, they need feedback. However, Millennials are looking for feedback delivered differently than with other generations.

Here's how to make a habit of giving Millennials effective feedback:

Be timely. Millennials are most engaged with daily contact with managers, either in a meeting, a quick face-to-face check-in, or from a phone call, text or email, according to a 2016 Gallup poll. That doesn't mean they need feedback every day or want to implement hard-and-fast rules for how often they get this feedback. The feeling is that it should occur organically. Managers will do best motivating Millennials if they get into the habit of letting them know as soon as possible whether they've done something wrong or something great.

Be honest. The stereotype is that Millennials have been so coddled by their parents that they must be sweet-talked in the workplace, but that's not true.

"Millennials are really good at cutting through the crap," says Christopher Farmer, a Millennial and Category Manager with Gap Inc. "If you are trying to gently say something to us, we see right through what you are trying to say, and we'd much prefer that you are just blunt and direct."

That doesn't mean be rude or inconsiderate. It means to be honest. State the truth as diplomatically and helpfully as possible, but be sure it's the truth. Millennials equate being told the truth with being shown respect, whereas doing the opposite makes them feel like they are being treated as sensitive children who need to be coddled. Being direct helps them to respect the judgment of the person speaking. Furthermore, being forthright and telling a Millennial when they've done something really well fosters a confidence in them. It also allows them to believe and trust what is being said. That translates into being proud of what they've accomplished. And that confidence will encourage them in everything they do going forward.

Avoid the feedback sandwich. Many managers believe that sandwiching criticism between two compliments will make their Millennial employees and themselves feel better. But this is not effective for a variety of reasons.

Imagine someone tells you a story, then asks you to repeat that story back to them as accurately as you can. What you'll remember best is the part at the beginning and the part at the end. In science, that's called the primacy effect and the recency effect. This means, as the research shows, that employees best remember comments stated at the beginning and at the end of a meeting. In a feedback sandwich, placing compliments between two criticisms tries to turn that research upside down hoping employees will remember the compliments sandwiched in the middle.

Ayelet Fishbach, a professor of behavioral science and marketing at the University of Chicago, has conducted simulations in her classes where students use the feedback sandwich to give each other constructive criticism about poor performance. When the students who received the feedback are surveyed later, they mistakenly thought they were doing great.

However, if you use the feedback sandwich consistently, your employees will catch on. They'll come to view your compliments as mere throwaways that are preludes to criticism. They'll feel suspicious and anxious while you're delivering praise, waiting for the other shoe to drop. In time, this will diminish the effect of any positive feedback, even when it's not followed by a critique.

Be empathetic. Millennials have grown up in an age, where people are much more self-aware and in tune with emotions than previous generations. The days of the emotionally tone-deaf boss are numbered. As workplaces become more circular, more familial, and more team-centric, aspects of emotional intelligence such as empathy are becoming even more essential.

Managers must be attuned to their employees' emotional state and body language, and then adjust the tenor of their feedback accordingly. Is the person clearly having a bad day and feeling demoralized? If so, that is not the right time to come down too hard on them. If the person seems receptive and eager to improve, then the astute manager can tell it to them straight and help them work out solutions.

These days, many managers are replacing the Golden Rule with the more empathetic Platinum Rule (the phrase coined by author Tony Alessandra): "Treat others the way they want to be treated." For example, a Gen X manager who doesn't need much feedback might prefer a CEO who maintains very little contact and gives her lots of freedom. So, if she follows the Golden Rule, she gives her Millennial staff very little feedback, believing she's giving them the kind of autonomy she would want in their position. And although her intentions are good, she may be inadvertently causing her Millennial employees to feel ignored, devalued, and uncertain. If she follows the Platinum Rule, she would ask each of her coworkers what kind of feedback they want and how often they need it, and then tailor her management behaviors to their needs.

Give actionable feedback. Scores of books and articles advise managers to give specific feedback. Yet vague feedback remains one of Millennials' most common complaints because it leaves them feeling uncertain and undervalued. One way to eliminate this feeling is to ensure your feedback is *actionable.* Before you give someone a critique, ask yourself if this information will allow the person to take a specific action to improve or if it will give them a specific solution. The same principle applies to giving positive feedback. If an employee does something well and you want them to repeat that action, be specific when you comment on that action. By saying "Great job on the presentation" does not allow someone to repeat the specific qualities that made the presentation great.

Ask for feedback on how you give feedback. Ask Millennial employees how you can improve the way you communicate both positive and negative feedback to them. Talk to fellow managers about the lessons they've learned. Ask trusted colleagues to let you know if, for example, you gave employees ineffective feedback during a meeting, and how you could rephrase your comments next time.

All the above strategies – PAR, goal-setting, and feedback – can be used in everyday, informal communication with Millennials to keep them engaged and motivated. These techniques can also be rolled into structured programs designed to help Millennials realize their full potential, including mentoring and leadership training.

It's now time to explore how to rethink mentoring programs for Millennials to maximize their success.

Make Mentoring More Circular

The mentor/protégé partnership is an ideal way to help Millennials learn and grow because it mirrors their family dynamic. Remember, many Millennials grew up in a circular family, where their parents, rather than acting as authority figures demanding things of an underling, fostered a more equal relationship that was all about nurturing, educating, and motivating.

Most corporations have mentoring programs in place, but they're often not effective for Millennials and their changing needs that include advancing technologies, flattening corporate structures, and shifting priorities.

Consider Various Types of Millennial Mentoring Programs

We're all familiar with the classic scenario: a veteran coaches a rookie. But there are other options that can be equally effective. Before you institute a mentoring program, first consider your main objective(s). Is it skills transference? Career planning? Familiarization with the company? Leadership development? Bridging generational gaps? Understanding your objectives will help you structure your mentoring program. If you have multiple goals, you might choose to set up two or three different mentoring programs. Below are brief descriptions of proven options.

Reverse Mentoring: Corporations including Hewlett-Packard, General Electric, and the advertising agency Ogilvy & Mather have all incorporated "reverse mentoring" programs. In these reverse programs, Millennials help Boomers and Gen Xers boost their technology and social media skills. They can also facilitate discussions around potentially outdated practices and present a fresh perspective. This practice also allows more seasoned employees to provide a practical viewpoint, impart the wisdom of their experience, and prepare Millennials for leadership roles. Reverse mentoring has proven to be an excellent way to bridge generational gaps and facilitate collaboration between generations.

Peer Mentoring: At Intel, each employee fills out a questionnaire, and then they're matched with peers throughout the country based on their skills. Mentors communicate via intranet or video chatting. This circular system is based on sharing ideas and collaborating nationwide, rather than on helping people rise through the ranks.

BT Group, the British telecommunications company, offers a modern peer mentoring program called Dare2Share. Employees create five- to 10-minute videos about skills or insights they've learned. Their coworkers can view the videos – plus read documents and participate in discussion threads – on the Dare2Share site and are able to connect with the "video mentor" if they want to learn more.

Network Mentoring: Host networking events and job shadowing to foster partnerships. Instead of – or in addition to – assigning Millennials a series of mentors, you can set up scenarios that help cultivate mentoring partnerships.

For example, Disney hosts meet-and-greets with employees from departments throughout the corporation to facilitate connections between people who don't normally work together. Following these events, the company offers job shadowing and temporary assignments so employees can closely observe and even briefly perform a different job. These practices are essentially mentoring programs in themselves, but they also foster potential long-term, informal mentoring relationships.

Train mentors and mentees. Just as it requires training to be a good manager and a good employee, it requires training to be a good mentor or mentee. Coach your mentors and mentees about your company's mentoring practices, the participants' roles, the program's goals, why mentoring is valuable, and how to get the most out of it. However, don't try to enforce rigid rules. Mentoring relationships are, first and foremost, relationships, and those work best when they develop naturally and informally.

Real World Example: Millennial-Friendly Mentoring at Fennemore Craig

James Goodnow is a shareholder at Fennemore Craig, a law firm founded when Grover Cleveland was president. Just imagine: suits, starched shirts, and "Yes, sirs." But James, and others, thought it could be different so they spoke up. Today, Fennemore Craig is at the forefront of adopting programs aimed at meeting the needs of Millennials workers, and it remains one of the most successful law firms in the country. Part of that success is due to its mentoring programs, which are continually evolving to adjust to the needs of Millennials and of the modern workplace.

In the firm's traditional mentoring program, new first-year associate lawyers are assigned an associate mentor and a partner mentor. Picks are made primarily based on the associate's focus of study in the law and how it matches the assignment at the practice, along with how well the associate's personality will be compatible with that of the mentor. Every year, associates have the choice of changing mentors or keeping their current mentors. There are no hard feelings if people switch and associates are encouraged to pick new mentors to get a variety of perspectives.

Though this formal program works well, the firm has found that when a shareholder takes someone under their wing, a stronger mentoring relationship develops organically. These mentoring relationships can arise through the traditional program, during the company's training programs, or via networking. In the firm's culture, shareholders are expected to mentor associates to help them with career and business development, succession planning, navigating the firm's political waters, and more.

But, like many large law firms, Fennemore Craig has found that some Millennial lawyers have inquired about tweaking the associate mentoring program, which is intended to help associates become firm shareholders. Though shareholders usually make more money, they face a challenging road that requires a lot of personal sacrifice, including but not limited to long hours in the office, attending various events, sometimes after work and on weekends, being on boards, and generating business outside of the office. For those reasons, some Millennial lawyers aren't interested in becoming shareholders.

They'd prefer to make less money to achieve a better quality of life. Because of this Millennial-driven paradigm shift, Fennemore Craig now employs many different categories of attorneys: practice group lawyers, contract lawyers, and "of counsel" lawyers. The firm is even exploring the idea of virtual lawyers who work from home. To meet the needs of these new categories of lawyers, they're in the process of adjusting the traditional mentoring model. In the meantime, lawyers in the informal mentoring process have stepped up and adapted to the changing Millennial mindset.

When you're working with and mentoring Millennials, you'll naturally observe their individual strengths, identify future leaders, and look for ways to develop their potential. But even the process of leadership development is changing in response to Millennials and to the requirements of the modern workplace.

Identifying Leaders in the Circular Company

As more companies become circular, and more job positions require complex thinking and innovation, the nature of leadership is changing. "In this new, flat structure of operation," says Jenny Poon of CO+HOOTS, "it basically calls for companies to have no low-level, entry-level positions. It calls for leadership in every role."

This means different styles of leadership will be necessary. In traditional triangular companies, the authoritarian leader typically rose to the top. This leadership style will always have a place in companies, and can be very successful. However, other leadership styles will also prove invaluable to circular, collaborative companies: democratic leaders who make sure everyone's input is valued; affiliative leaders who create harmony between coworkers; coaches who can motivate their teams; and, most importantly, leaders who can adopt all of these management styles as needed.

With leadership skills required in all positions, it's essential to identify Millennial leaders early and start training them for their futures – now.

IDENTIFYING ATTRIBUTES FOR MILLENNIAL LEADERS OF THE FUTURE

Look for qualities not classically associated with leadership. Because of circular upbringings, Millennials are less likely to be authoritarian leaders and more likely to exhibit leadership qualities suited to collaborative environments.

For example, you might work with a Millennial who's great at bringing out the best in their coworkers, praising their strengths and motivating them to excel. That's the coaching style of leadership and it can be successful, particularly in a business that is organized with numerous small teams.

Another Millennial might have a knack for nurturing relationships between coworkers, fostering harmony, and creating a family atmosphere in the company. This is the affiliative style of leadership, and sadly, it's underrated. That needs to change, because it's ideal for building the bonds of trust that facilitate innovative thinking, creativity, risk-taking, and adaptability.

Yet another Millennial might be a big-picture thinker who's passionate about the company's mission. This person could be trained to inspire and motivate the staff, becoming an excellent visionary leader. Many Millennials possess several of these qualities – or could be taught how and when to employ each of these management styles.

Look for "I will" instead of IQ. University of Pennsylvania psychologist Angela Lee Duckworth has studied a wide variety of people: cadets in West Point Military Academy, salespeople in private companies, teachers in tough neighborhoods, and contestants in the National Spelling Bee. In each case, she and her team asked, "Who is the most successful, and why?" The characteristic that emerged as a significant predictor of success was not IQ. It was grit, passion, perseverance, and the willingness to stand up and say "I will."

Millennials with "I will" always take initiative and go the extra mile. They're mission-driven. They seek out opportunities to learn and grow. They're engaged and present.

Millennials with "I will" always take initiative and go the extra mile. They're mission-driven. They seek out opportunities to learn and grow. They're engaged and present. Millennials are not the ones checking their phones throughout every meeting. They are catalysts of change; they don't sit around saying, "That's someone else's responsibility." They can even be exhausting and annoying sometimes. Like Socrates' gadfly, they're always questioning the status quo and motivating themselves and others to do better.

These Millennials could make great leaders.

Look for "EI" (Emotional Intelligence). EI embodies some of the qualities of "I will," but adds to them. Emotional intelligence includes self-awareness (understanding your feelings, strengths and weaknesses); self-management (the ability to control your emotions); self-motivation; empathy; and social skills that help a person build relationships, persuade, and motivate people.

Although these qualities are sometimes referred to as "soft" skills, in reality, there is nothing soft about them.

In 1996, Harvard psychology professor David McClellan studied division leaders at an international food and beverage company. He found that managers who scored high on several EI factors were more successful – not just in creating a happier work environment, but also in generating profits. Their departments exceeded annual revenue targets by 15 to 20 percent, whereas the divisions run by directors who scored low on EI underperformed by nearly 20 percent.

Millennials demand leaders with EI, and want to be leaders with emotional intelligence. What's more, increasingly collaborative and circular businesses also require leaders with high emotional intelligence.

HOW TO SPOT MILLENNIALS WITH EI

Millennials with EI will exhibit these or similar qualities:

- Millennials who are self-aware and take responsibility for their actions. They speak candidly and have integrity. They are open to critique and acknowledge areas they need to improve. They understand that the ability to point out one's own weaknesses is a strength, not weakness.

- Millennials who manage their emotions and maintain composure during times of stress. Though they may be passionate about their mission, they also have the ability to step back and calmly analyze a situation. On the other hand, the employee who sends out angry emails in the heat of emotion is not good at self-management. Abraham Lincoln wrote numerous angry letters to his political enemies, but he never sent them. They were found in a drawer after his death. That's self-discipline. And it's great leadership.

- Millennials with empathy and social skills. They're well-liked by a wide variety of people. But this doesn't necessarily mean they're the life of the party; plenty of introverts are well-liked and skilled at leadership. They're optimistic and positive, but also realistic. They care about their coworkers and thoughtfully consider their feelings. They also care about the company's customers and try to look at things from their perspective. This engaging Millennial type is easy to spot.

Multicultural Millennials with EI

Watch out for your own unconscious biases. Picture a leader. What's the first image that pops into your head? For some, it's a white man. He's probably also heterosexual, reasonably tall, and of medium build. The image in your mind doesn't indicate anything about your personality. It just means that over a lifetime, your unconscious mind has noticed and filed away thousands of images under the mental category of "leader," and most of them fit that description. So your mental "stock image" of a leader may not be female, LGBT, Hispanic, African-American, petite or overweight, or multi-tattooed.

The brain's tendency toward mental shorthand can nudge us in certain directions when it comes to identifying and promoting potential leaders. And it's not just a white male thing. The "like me" bias sometimes leads managers to promote people who look like them, or who are in their own image.

These unconscious biases are particularly worrisome because Millennials are the most diverse generation America has ever seen. Baby Boomers age 55 and older are 75 percent white; while Millennials are just 55 percent white. More Millennials are openly LGBT. (And 40 percent have tattoos.) Since Millennials will occupy most leadership roles by 2030, companies nationwide should see their most diverse collection of leaders ever. That means Millennials will be challenging and changing the mental "stock image" of a leader. When identifying and promoting leaders, managers must be aware of their unconscious biases and make an effort to evaluate Millennials on our merits.

Training: Managers vs. Motivators

Just as the nature of leadership is changing, the goal of leadership training must change. Numerous books and articles talk about managing Millennials. But anytime you hear that triangular phrase, it should set off warnings. Millennials do not want to be managed. Nor are they inclined to be managers in the traditional sense. In fact, the title "manager" has to go. A manager is responsible for controlling a part of a company or organization. No Millennial wants to feel controlled or to be expected to control others.

Instead, Millennials want to be motivated and to be motivators. To Millennials, the word *motivation* is related to the words motive and move. A motivator gives people reasons or motives to move or to take action. A motivator galvanizes and inspires the people around them.

So the goal of leadership training cannot be to groom Millennials to be managers. Instead, the goal of leadership training should be to empower Millennials to be motivators.

STEPS FOR THINKING LIKE A MOTIVATOR (INSTEAD OF A MANAGER)

Empower Millennials to be intrapreneurs. An intrapreneur acts like an entrepreneur, but within a corporate structure. An intrapreneur is given the autonomy to innovate and become a leader in their own corporate arena.

"I think Millennials in general are looking to leave their little mark on the world, whether that's by building their own company or creating a new process," says Jenny Poon. "So I think that essentially taking away this top-down structure, empowering every single person to be an innovator in their organization and to lead and own their own pieces of the business is what creates a very high-functioning, efficient team. As long as you're still able to accomplish a majority of what you intended to do, you should have time to dream and explore, and be the leader in your own industry, in your own world."

Some companies – such as 3M, Google and Hewlett-Packard – encourage intrapreneurship by using programs known as "15 percent time" or "20 percent time." These programs allow employees to use a portion of their paid time to dream up products, invent solutions, and pursue projects of their own choosing. This may seem like an invitation to slack off, but in reality, employees have hatched some of the companies' most successful endeavors during this autonomous free time. A 3M scientist invented the Post-It note during his 15 percent time. A Google engineer used his 20 percent time to create Gmail.

Educate Millennials incrementally, not annually. Just as the annual review and annual bonus are not effective for motivating Millennials, an annual leadership training session is not sufficient to grow Millennials into motivators. Leadership doesn't happen once a year in a formal classroom setting; it happens every day, on the job. So motivational leadership training should happen consistently and frequently, and both formally and informally. It should be woven into your company's culture and used as a regular feature of your feedback sessions.

Teach Millennials to motivate themselves. Leaders must lead by example, so if Millennials are going to motivate others, they must first motivate themselves. That can be challenging, even for naturally enthusiastic people. It's easy to get caught up in day-to-day tasks and deadlines, and lose sight of the big picture. Motivators must constantly point their mental compass toward the company's mission as well as their personal purpose. They must set short-term and long-term goals for themselves and maintain a positive attitude around their team. That doesn't mean they should be fake; but if a motivator has a bad day, they must put others before themselves and think, "I'm not going to let my bad day have a negative impact on the people around me. It's my job to keep everyone inspired."

Teach Millennials to motivate individuals. Millennials may be team-focused, but motivators can't be effective simply by giving rousing speeches in the conference room. Every person who is part of a team has specific goals, values, and interests that motivate them. So motivators must get to know each person on the team, learn what drives them, and take a different approach to motivating every one of those individuals. They must focus on each person's purpose and work with them to set and achieve their specific goals.

To accomplish this, it's important to teach Millennials effective communication skills. They must learn how to get an idea across clearly, simply, and engagingly – whether they're in face-to-face meetings, emailing, posting something on social media, or shooting a video.

Teach Millennials critical thinking. It's no good having a leader who can galvanize people to pursue a plan if that plan has no merit in the first place. Millennials (and people from every generation) must be taught to research the pros and cons of their proposals, reason through the potential consequences of these actions, provide evidence for their assumptions, and be willing to prove themselves wrong or be proved wrong by others.

Encourage Millennials to reach beyond their position. Christopher Farmer of Gap says his best boss "was always encouraging us to reach beyond our job titles or our job descriptions. He was never one to say, 'This is your responsibility, this is your role, and don't step outside that.'"

Managers tell people to perform the responsibilities of their job position, but motivators encourage and empower people to be the best they can be, to think outside the box and strive for excellence.

Managers tell people to perform the responsibilities of their job position, but motivators encourage and empower people to be the best they can be, to think outside the box and strive for excellence. To do this, motivators must show their employees that they trust them. Motivators must give their employees space to succeed or fail. And they must train Millennials to one day become the motivators who give their employees the same trust and encouragement.

THE FREEDOM TO SUCCEED

Throughout this book, we've drawn parallels between family and work dynamics. Nowhere is that more true than when you're helping your Millennial employees realize their full potential. Think of it like raising a workplace family, in a circular business just like in your circular household. Just as you want your children to learn and to grow into the best people they can be, you also want your coworkers to learn and to grow into the best they can be. If your children make a mistake, you point out their errors, explain the potential consequences, and steer them in the right direction. The same approach holds true for giving feedback to your staff. You give your children the freedom to try and to fail, but you also alert them if they're about to fail too seriously. Your Millennial employees need the same kind of freedom. You want your children to aim high and achieve more than you ever did. And you have the power to help your workplace family aim high and achieve more than they ever dreamed possible. By doing so, by giving this kind of permission and freedom, your company and its staff, Millennials, Gen Xers, and Baby Boomers, will achieve more than you ever dreamed.

Real-World Story: Gen Xer Perspective
Mindy Miller, Director of Destination Sales at
JW Marriott San Antonio Hill Country Resort & Spa

"If you take care of the associate, the associate will take care of the guest, and then everyone's happy."

From a young age, Gen Xer Mindy Miller was schooled in psychology. Her mother has a degree in the subject, and she taught Miller how to pick up clues about people's personalities and understand their motivations. Maybe that's why Miller approaches her career with such emotional intelligence. She creates a family atmosphere in her workplace and even shares a percentage of her annual bonus with her staff. "I ask a lot of them, and I just don't feel right that I collect a bonus and they don't, just because they're hourly and I'm salaried," she says. "I wouldn't have gotten to where I was without them, because their success is my success, and vice versa."

What else does Miller do to keep her staff motivated?

TAKE CARE OF PEOPLE: "The foundation on which Marriott was built is the belief that if you take care of the associate, the associate will take care of the guest, and then everyone's happy," Miller says. "And that, I think, causes people to stay longer. I think anytime you feel a part of something bigger than you, it makes you happy. There is an emotional connection that makes it less of a job, and you see more potential for a career, particularly when you have some successes under you belt and you feel appreciated."

BE EMPATHETIC: "I don't necessarily make a conscious effort to define myself compared to Millennials," Miller says. "I just try to put myself in their shoes and imagine what they would want to know about what the expectations of a job are. I just think you ought to treat people equally. You need to be respectful and remember how intimidating your first full-time jobs were."

GIVE EMPLOYEES THE FREEDOM TO MAKE DECISIONS: "I think Marriott empowers their associates to make decisions with regard to their role and how it can benefit the guest. There aren't restrictions put on what you can do. You ultimately just want to make the customer happy and do right by them. So Marriott doesn't try to micromanage and tell us how to do it. It's more a case of, 'Do what you think is right.'"

SEE PAST THE STEREOTYPES: "You hear all the time that Millennials have a sense of entitlement and don't want to put in the work or the time to advance, and that they just want it now. I've hired probably six or seven Millennials for our destination sales coordinator role. And I have found they've worked harder. I think they know that the position is going to be a launching pad, and that if they do well in that role, it'll be an entree into management. So I think that if you communicate the expectations and you've found somebody with some character, there isn't any sense of entitlement or wanting some of the perks that come with my job."

BE A MENTOR: "I'm seen as a mentor, who has certain expectations about what the job entails. My staff and the people I mentor know they can come to me, and I want them to tell me what they're thinking, as well as what positions interest them. I sit down with them and help them list the pros and cons, as well as their next step in life, or where are they personally. I ask them if that aligns with where they want to be."

TAKEAWAY QUESTIONS:

- Are you taking care of your staff, so that they, in turn, take care of your customers?
- Are you empowering your staff to make their own decisions about how to approach a goal?
- Are you regularly talking with your staff about their career and life goals?

ABOUT THE AUTHORS

Ryan Avery is one of the Millennial generation's most profound speakers on generational leadership and strategic communication. At age 25, Ryan became the youngest World Champion of Public Speaking in history, competing against more than 30,000 contestants from 116 countries to claim the 2012 World Championship for Toastmasters International.

Ryan has delivered keynotes on every continent in the world, is an Emmy-award winning journalist, and a best-selling author. Ryan currently lives in Denver, Colorado with his wife, Chelsea, and daughter, Atlas. He is a highly sought-after headliner at conferences and for conducting company-wide trainings on the power of strategic communication between generations.

Learn more about Ryan at: **www.RyanAvery.com**

James Goodnow has been named one of *"America's Techiest Lawyers"* and has gained national recognition as the face of the Millennial generation in business. As one of the youngest senior leaders in a major US Law rm, the Harvard Law School graduate is a go-to source for the media for topics related to Millennials in business.

James is also a well-known legal commentator who has appeared on or been covered by CNN, Good Morning America, Today, the Wall Street Journal, the Washington Post, People Magazine and many other national media outlets. James lives with his wife and kids in Phoenix, Arizona.

Learn more about James at: **www.JamesGoodnow.com**

CPSIA information can be obtained
at www.ICGtesting.com
Printed in the USA
LVOW05*2347210617
538961LV00023B/762/P